SUPERNATU

GJERTRUD SCHNACKENBERG was born in 1953. Her include fellowships from the Guggenheim Foundation and the National Endowment for the Arts, the Rome Prize in Literature, and an Award in Literature from the American Academy of Arts and Letters. She has been a Christensen Visiting Fellow at St. Catherine's College, Oxford, and a Visiting Scholar at the Getty Research Institute for the History of Art and the Humanities. She is also the author of *The Throne of Labdacus*.

BY GJERTRUD SCHNACKENBERG

Portraits and Elegies (1982)

The Lamplit Answer (1985)

A Gilded Lapse of Time (1992)

The Throne of Labdacus (2000)

SUPERNATURAL LOVE

POEMS 1976–1992

GJERTRUD
SCHNACKENBERG

Farrar, Straus and Giroux

NEW YORK

FARRAR, STRAUS AND GIROUX
18 West 18th Street, New York 10011

Distributed in Canada by D&M Publishing, Inc.
Printed in the United States of America
First edition, 2000

Grateful acknowledgment is made to *Antaeus*, *The Atlantic*, *The Carolina
Quarterly*, *The Kenyon Review*, *The Mississippi Review*, *The New Yorker*, *The
Paris Review*, *Ploughshares*, *Poetry*, and *The Yale Review*, where some of
these poems first appeared. *Portraits and Elegies* was first published in
1982 by David R. Godine, Publisher, Inc.

Library of Congress Cataloging-in-Publication Data
Schnackenberg, Gjertrud.
    Supernatural love : poems 1976–1992 / Gjertrud Schnackenberg.
      p.   cm.
    ISBN-13: 978-0-374-52754-9 (alk. paper)
    ISBN-10: 0-374-52754-7 (alk. paper)
    I. Title.

PS3569.C5178 S36 2000
811'.54—dc21

                                        00037564

Designed by Gretchen Achilles

www.fsgbooks.com

14 13 12 11 10 9 8 7 6 5

FOR MY MOTHER

CONTENTS

PORTRAITS

AND

ELEGIES

(1982)

☀

FOR MY MOTHER
AND IN MEMORY OF
MY FATHER

LAUGHING

WITH

ONE EYE

(1977)

WALTER CHARLES SCHNACKENBERG

PROFESSOR OF HISTORY

(1917 - 1973)

And call those works extravagance of breath
That are not suited for such men as come
Proud, open-eyed and laughing to the tomb.
W. B. YEATS, *"Vacillation"*

1. NIGHTFISHING

The kitchen's old-fashioned planter's clock portrays
A smiling moon as it dips down below
Two hemispheres, stars numberless as days,
And peas, tomatoes, onions, as they grow
Under that happy sky; but though the sands
Of time put on this vegetable disguise,
The clock covers its face with long, thin hands.
Another smiling moon begins to rise.

We drift in the small rowboat an hour before
Morning begins, the lake weeds grown so long
They touch the surface, tangling in an oar.
You've brought coffee, cigars, and me along.
You sit still, like a monument in a hall,
Watching for trout. A bat slices the air
Near us, I shriek, you look at me, that's all,
One long sobering look, a smile everywhere
But on your mouth. The mighty hills shriek back.
You turn back to the lake, chuckle, and clamp
Your teeth on your cigar. We watch the black
Water together. Our tennis shoes are damp.
Something moves on your thoughtful face, recedes.
Here, for the first time ever, I see how,
Just as a fish lurks deep in water weeds,
A thought of death will lurk deep down, will show
One eye, then quietly disappear in you.
It's time to go. Above the hills I see
The faint moon slowly dipping out of view,
Sea of Tranquillity, Sea of Serenity,
Ocean of Storms . . . You start to row, the boat

Skimming the lake where light begins to spread.
You stop the oars, midair. We twirl and float.

I'm in the kitchen. You are three days dead.
A smiling moon rises on fertile ground,
White stars and vegetables. The sky is blue.
Clock hands sweep by it all, they twirl around,
Pushing me, oarless, from the shore of you.

2. INTERMEZZO

Steinway in German script above the keys,
Letters like dragons curling stiff gold tails,
Gold letters, ivory keys, the black wood cracked
By years of sunlight, into dragon scales.
Your music breathed its fire into the room.
We'd hear jazz sprouting thistles of desire,
Or jazz like the cat's cry from beneath
The passing tire, when you played the piano
Afternoons; or "Au Clair de la Lune."
Scarlatti's passages fluttered like pages.
Sometimes you turned to Brahms, a depth, more true,
You studied him to find out how he turned
Your life into a memory for you.

In Number 6 of Opus 1 1 8,
Such brief directions, Andante, *sotto voce*:
The opening notes like single water drops
Each with an oceanic undertow
That pulled you deeper even as you surfaced
Hundreds of miles from where the first note drew
You in, and made your life a memory,
Something that happened long ago to you.

And through that Intermezzo you could see
As through a two-way mirror, until it seemed
You looked back at your life as at a room,
And saw those images that would compose
Your fraction of eternity, the hallway
In its absolute repose, the half-lit room,
The drapes at evening holding the scent of heat,

The marble long-lost under the piano,
A planet, secretive, cloud-wrapped, and blue,
Silent and gorgeous by your foot, making
A god lost in reflection, a god of you.

3 . WALKING HOME

Walking home from school one afternoon,
Slightly abstracted, what were you thinking of?
Turks in Vienna? Luther on Christian love?
Or were you with Van Gogh beneath the moon
With candles in his hatband, painting stars
Like singed hairs spinning in a candle flame?
Or giant maps where men take, lose, reclaim
Whole continents with pins? Or burning cars
And watchtowers and army-censored news
In Chile, in the Philippines, in Greece,
Colonels running the universities,
Assassinations, executions, coups—

You walked, and overhead some pipsqueak bird
Flew by and dropped a lot of something that
Splattered, right on the good professor, splat.
Now, on the ancient Rhine, so Herod heard,
The old Germanic chieftains always read
Such droppings as good luck: opening the door,
You bowed to improve my view of what you wore,
So luckily, there on the center of your head.

Man is not a god, that's what you said
After your heart gave out, to comfort me
Who came to comfort you but sobbed to see
Your heartbeat zigzagging on a TV overhead.
You knew the world was in a mess, and so,
By God, were you; and yet I never knew
A man who loved the world as much as you,
And that love was the last thing to let go.

4 . A DREAM

Death makes of your abandoned face
A secret house an empty place
And I come back wanting that much
To ask you to come back I touch

The door where are you it's so black
The taste of smoke is smoke I back
Away when creeping lines of fire
Appear and travel faster higher

Where are you and beneath the floor
God turns the gas jets up they soar
The way flames soar and I should run
And blackness burning like the sun

All empty underneath my hair
I start to chuckle where oh where
My brimming eyes don't understand
I press my grin against my hand

5 . BAVARIA

That day in Germany comes back, the deep
Enchanted woods and Castle Neuschwanstein,
A clouded mind's fantastical decline
To fairy-tale dream halls. The barren steep
Mountain of rock behind the torrent as it drops
To silver thunder, the path of our approach
Built for his lit-up French rococo coach,
Clouds, alps, towers, stack like theater props
Around the locked gates where his guards defied
Psychiatrists from Munich. And as we look
Into a courtyard from a storybook,
You describe what we would find inside:

Romanticism's last hysteria
Of Niebelungen murals golden-iced
Along the Hall of Song, the King with Christ
Floating in gold above Bavaria,
Chambers where every fantasy is wooed,
A cave of artificial stalactites
And waterfalls lit by electric lights,
The Throne Room where, in mountain solitude,

Ludwig the Second works a Ouija board.
His tongue searches a cavity, he relishes
The nerve and pain, das Reich as far off as
The twangling of a cloudscaped harpsichord.
The heroes of the ancient race festoon
This dream theater, this lunatic's refuge
And lovers' hideaway, this whole weird huge
Orbit of Wagner's artificial moon . . .

Cosima sniffs a "new brutality
In men," now that Wagner is dead, his music's
Tree of lightning bears a politics
Of acid fruit; and blanket-wrapped Nietzsche
Sees armies marching out of village clocks
From where he sits in Zurich's health resort,
His nightmare coming true, the fresh report
Of shrill fringes expounding paradox
In Viennese cafés, where young men slake
Their power thirst with "primacy of will,"
Like heroes, in a castle, on a hill . . .
The Dream King floating face down on the lake.

You say, Time will be fair; but I see how
The West gathers, how all the diseased West
Could crush you, like a pressure in the chest
Building, decade by decade, toward Dachau,
Toward hiding places flushed by midnight knocks:
A woman bends in futile reflex to
Conceal her wedding diamonds in her shoe,
They hurt her foot, her panicked hand unlocks
The door, she finds, not the police, but her
Sister-in-law, looking left and right,
The coarse face underlined by a soft white
Collar of newly confiscated fur,
The paws intact, "Still, I've a heart, yes,
That I have," furtive on the landing.
Now, somewhere the Hangman of Stutthof is handing
A Todeskandidat a paper dress;
As camp by camp the lawless ego maps

The growing territory it proclaims,
A small eraser rubs a list of names
To rubber bits; now, as the Führer naps,
Dreaming of Wild Westerns in his chair
Till early morning, now, in North Berlin,
An apartment building shatters from within,
And, like a tooth, a bathtub dangles there.

We linger, for a moment, at the gates:
Here Ludwig, in his grisly innocence,
Plucked water lilies planted an hour since
By silent gardeners, hurled his dinner plates
At statue niches peopled with assassins,
And wept that Nietzsche called his love a Jew.
It is November 1962,
A siren from the village rises, spins
Itself into a planet of alarm
That hangs a moment in the wilderness,
And dusk comes through the forest with Venus,
Star of emergency, upon its arm.

6. THE BICYCLIST

Crossing a bridge in our VW bus
In Stratford-on-Avon, you swerved but grazed
A skinny man riding a bicycle.
God! Was he mad! You pulled off to the side
Beyond the bridge, and he came after us
Shouting, Police! and pedaling furiously
In his black suit. You stood by the bus
As he pulled up and flailed at his kickstand
And rained vituperation on your head.
You quietly cut through his narrative,
"Are you all right?" your face kindly and wry.

Through the bus window I saw the moment when
He first saw you, first looked you in the eye.
He straightened up. His hands moved fast
To straighten his bow tie. Well, yes, he supposed
That he was fine. You asked more questions, asked
So quietly I couldn't hear, but I could see
His more emphatically respectful answers
As he began to nod in affirmation
Of all you said. Then he smiled, sort of,
Offering his hand, and when he pedaled off
He waved and shouted, Thank you very much!

That's what you were like—you could sideswipe
A bow-tied Englishman wobbling across
A narrow bridge on his collapsible bike,
And inspire him, somehow, to thank you for it.

7. A DREAM

In dreams silent secret and unafraid
I steal away to find you I've divined
Your wish to see me I steal away to find
You in a forest digging with a spade
I touch your shoulder feeling my heart race
To think how gladdened how surprised you'll be
To find me here I say Daddy it's me
I'm here I'll lead you back out of this place
Hurry but you don't speak and worse it seems
A feat of strength for you to turn this way
As if groping once and for all to say
There's nothing left nothing even in dreams
Only this face abandoned by your soul
This shade rooted beside a senseless hole
I fled through sleep to find you yes but this
This sightless face this crumbling blank and deep
Abyss where now I lay me down to sleep
Oh Lord You overwhelm the fatherless

8. RETURNING NORTH

The car lurches on goat paths,
North on north,
You ask shepherds directions as you drive.
Above the Arctic Circle
Norway's sun rises all night
On you bringing your family on your search
To meet your background face to face.
Your mother left in 1895,
A four-year-old Norwegian, steerage class,
Clutching a copper teapot in the hold,
Her one possession.
At forty-six
You come back as a dead sister's only son.

Your aged aunt waits at a pasture gate,
Holding your letter, looking anxious, small,
Shy as the summer snow
In patches at her feet.
You see your dead mother,
Her hands, her face, her raven hair, her eyes,
You see her hesitate.
She backs away, half frightened of our car,
And beckons us to follow her
Through cold summer meadows to a barn.
One by one we scale
A ladder and pull ourselves
Up through a hole in the ceiling
Above the pigs and geese,
We have arrived,
And there, lying upon a bed of straw,

A man stares, fever-eyed, then turns away.
Out of respect
The scared, exhilarated family
Hides whispering behind the kitchen door,
Peeking in turns to see
These rich Americans. Two children
Push each other into the room,
Their dialect is difficult for you.
They offer us
A plate of fish, a plate of goat cheese, bread
Which we are meant to eat in front of them,
Among the coughing and the shining eyes.
This would have been your mother's home.
And we begin to eat
Moments before you realize
The little household is tubercular.

Almost at once, you say that we must go,
There in the mountains
Days and days away,
You say our family is expected
Somewhere else, somewhere immediately,
You ask them to believe
Our visit has been good,
We must go south. They do not understand.
They pull at us, they watch us drive away,
Slowly, painfully south, finding
The way as tears will find their way
Into a mouth, hundreds of miles
To Oslo, the city of clean air

And Lutheran chapels stark, narrow, and pure,
And small, and white,
So like your mother's face.

You said lightly, Forget this incident.
But, Father, here, tonight,
It comes to mind
Or my mind comes to it as one winding
Through passageways cut through
Snow-covered sculptured hedges
Comes upon
A waterfall suspended in white frost
And stands amazed and lost, so am I
Lost remembering
The fear crossing your face.

9 . ROME

Behind the drapes and thousand-year-old door
We strained to see beyond the chapel's grille
And saw nothing but shadow shapes until
Our eyes adjusted. Then Demon and Whore
Rose on one wall, roaring for Beelzebub,
And dragged their fingernails through obscene crowds.
But rings of saints chanting in frescoed clouds
Gazed upward from the other wall, they rubbed
Their fingertips on Mary's hem. You stood
Alone a moment, your figure partly hid
Among those figures; and seeing you amid
That opulence of death, I understood
The wooden crucifix with Christ portrayed
Sagging in fear and in his downcast eyes
His sudden knowledge that to recognize
One's father, Father, is to be afraid.

10. WINTER APPLES

I open the kitchen window like an eye:
Our hearts hang in the naked apple boughs
All tumbledown with worms that grind and cry,
Sisters, it's time that one of you takes down

The dead man's clothes blown stiff upon the line.
He isn't here. And now his laughter stops
Rattling the teacups, now his tears, not mine,
Drip from my chin onto the countertop,

Little mirrors of that summertime we saw
An August evening's metamorphosis:
On our hot porch, a snake unhinged his jaw,
A toad half swallowed in his fatal kiss,

Twin heads and double tongue that cursed our door.
Now apples black with frost cling to the bough,
And all around this house the cold grass stirs
And breathes that frog's blue sob, Oh take me now.

11. A DREAM

With shadow ink, on paper that I know
Is shadow, I now make
An Arctic shadow world and ship to take
A last passage. The snow
Breaks up as though the shadow ship were there.
A man leaning against the rail

Watches the twilight North, a wail
Rises around me everywhere,
I realize
What I fear most is true,
That this is you.
And now I want to know, and my voice cries
Crying your name,

But when you turn to me, I find
Being alive is being left behind.
And being dead comes to the same.
Your pathway closes in the water

Among drifting ice continents.
I want to say you're not alone,
That I am here, to say I am your daughter,
But, instead, I stare the way you stare,

And marveling, I watch the face you wear,
Hardened into remote indifference,
Become my own.

12. "THERE ARE NO DEAD"

Outside, a phoebe whistles for its mate,
The rhododendron rubs its leaves against
Your office window: so the spring we sensed
You wouldn't live to see comes somewhat late.
Here, lying on the desk, your reading glasses,
And random bits of crimped tobacco leaves,
Your jacket dangling its empty sleeves—
These look as if you've just left for your classes.
The chess game is suspended on its board
In your mind's pattern, your wastebasket
Contains some crumpled papers, your filing cabinet
Is packed with years of writing working toward
A metaphysics of impersonal praise.
Here students came and went, here years would draw
Intensities of lines until we saw
Your face beneath an etching of your face.
How many students really cared to solve
History's riddles?—in hundreds on the shelves,
Where men trying to think about themselves
Must come to grips with grief that won't resolve,
Blackness of headlines in the daily news,
And buildings blown away from flights of stairs
All over Europe, tanks in empty squares,
The burning baby carriages of Jews.

Behind thin glass, a print hangs on the wall,
A detail from the Bayeux Tapestry.
As ignorant women gabbed incessantly,
Their red, sore hands stitched crudely to recall

Forests of ships, the star with streaming hair,
God at Westminster blessing the devout,
They jabbed their thousand needles in and out,
Sometimes too busy talking to repair
The small mistakes; now the centuries of grease
And smoke that stained it, and the blind white moth
And grinning worm that spiraled through the cloth,
Say death alone makes life a masterpiece.

There William of Normandy remounts his horse
A fourth time, four times desperate to drive
Off rumors of his death. His sword is drawn.
He swivels and lifts his visor up and roars,
Look at me well! For I am still alive!
Your glasses, lying on the desk, look on.

DARWIN

IN 1881

(1978)

☀

Sleepless as Prospero back in his bedroom
In Milan, with all his miracles
Reduced to sailors' tales,
He sits up in the dark. The islands loom.
His seasickness upwells,
Silence creeps by in memory as it crept
By him on water, while the sailors slept,
From broken eggs and vacant tortoise shells.
His voyage around the cape of middle age
Comes, with a feat of insight, to a close,
The same way Prospero's
Ended before he left the stage
To be led home across the blue-white sea,
When he had spoken of the clouds and globe,
Breaking his wand, and taking off his robe:
Knowledge increases unreality.

He quickly dresses.
Form wavers like his shadow on the stair
As he descends, in need of air
To cure his dizziness,
Down past the ship-sunk emptiness
Of grownup children's rooms and hallways where
The family portraits stare,
All haunted by each other's likenesses.

Outside, the orchard and a piece of moon
Are islands, he an island as he walks,
Brushing against weed stalks.
By hook and plume

The seeds gathering on his trouser legs
Are archipelagoes, like nests he sees
Shadowed in branching, ramifying trees,
Each with unique expressions in its eggs.
Different islands conjure
Different beings; different beings call
From different isles. And after all
His scrutiny of Nature
All he can see
Is how it will grow small, fade, disappear,
A coastline fading from a traveler
Aboard a survey ship. Slowly,
As coasts depart,
Nature had left behind a naturalist
Bound for a place where species don't exist,
Where no emergence has a counterpart.

He's heard from friends
About the other night, the banquet hall
Ringing with bravos—like a curtain call,
He thinks, when the performance ends,
Failing to summon from the wings
An actor who had lost his taste for verse,
Having beheld, in larger theaters,
Much greater banquet vanishings
Without the quaint device and thunderclap
Required in Act 3.
He wrote, Let your indulgence set me free,
To the Academy, and took a nap
Beneath a *London Daily* tent,

Then puttered on his hothouse walk
Watching his orchids beautifully stalk
Their unreturning paths, where each descendant
Is the last—
Their inner staircases
Haunted by vanished insect faces
So tiny, so intolerably vast.
And while they gave his proxy the award,
He dined in Downe and stayed up rather late
For backgammon with his beloved mate,
Who reads his books and is, quite frankly, bored.

Now done with beetle jaws and beaks of gulls
And bivalve hinges, now, utterly done,
One miracle remains, and only one.
An ocean swell of sickness rushes, pulls,
He leans against the fence
And lights a cigarette and deeply draws,
Done with fixed laws,
Done with experiments
Within his greenhouse heaven where
His offspring, Frank, for half the afternoon
Played, like an awkward angel, his bassoon
Into the humid air
So he could tell
If sound would make a Venus's-flytrap close.
And, done for good with scientific prose,
That raging hell
Of tortured grammars writhing on their stakes,

He'd turned to his memoirs, chuckling to write
About his boyhood in an upright
Home: a boy preferring garter snakes
To schoolwork, a lazy, strutting liar
Who quite provoked her aggravated look,
Shushed in the drawing room behind her book,
His bossy sister itching with desire
To tattletale—yes, that was good.
But even then, much like the conjurer
Grown cranky with impatience to abjure
All his gigantic works and livelihood
In order to immerse
Himself in tales where he could be the man
In Once upon a time there was a man,

He'd quite by chance beheld the universe:
A disregarded game of chess
Between two love-dazed heirs
Who fiddle with the tiny pairs
Of statues in their hands, while numberless
Abstract unseen
Combinings on the silent board remain
Unplayed forever when they leave the game
To turn, themselves, into a king and queen.
Now, like the coming day,
Inhaled smoke illuminates his nerves.
He turns, taking the sand walk as it curves
Back to the yard, the house, the entranceway
Where, not to waken her,

He softly shuts the door,
And leans against it for a spell before
He climbs the stairs, holding the banister,
Up to their room: there
Emma sleeps, moored
In illusion, blown past the storm he conjured
With his book, into a harbor
Where it all comes clear,
Where island beings leap from shape to shape
As to escape
Their terrifying turns to disappear.
He lies down on the quilt,
He lies down like a fabulous-headed
Fossil in a vanished riverbed,
In ocean drifts, in canyon floors, in silt,
In lime, in deepening blue ice,
In cliffs obscured as clouds gather and float;
He lies down in his boots and overcoat,
And shuts his eyes.

19

HADLEY

STREET

(1976)

✺

Even the sparrow finds a home,
and the swallow a nest for herself,
where she may lay her young,
at thy altar, O Lord my God.
        —Psalm 84:3

1. DUSTING

A circle widens beneath my cloth, the years
Of dust rubbed from the wavy windowpanes.
Bits of planets, burst stars have sifted down,
Dust from remote globes of the universe
Drops in our closets, piles in corners softly,
Swirls in sunrays toward boxes we'll unpack,
Around the clocks and mirrors under sheets;
The clouds I shake from carpets give it back,

The children paste paper stars upon the door.
With wet footprints disappearing in the hall,
Old wallpaper designs disclosing faces,
The faucet's voice, the floorboard's startled cry
Under my heel, what ghost is it accounts
For breath in the rooms, pale tears coursing
The windowpanes, what ghosts? I count even
The doorknob in my hand among the living.

2. ELIZABETH AND EBEN, 1960

The windows framed her, watching, and the doors:
Here she was born, she brought her husband here
And loved him, lived with him through two world wars,
Ignorant as he was, ox-strong, eyes clear
As water, simple, tender, handy, Christian.
After they found out, he rarely spoke,
She drove him home after the operation.
He sweated through the sheets that night, then woke

And dressed, and watched her make their morning coffee.
He sharpened a pencil with a kitchen knife,
Letting the shavings curl around his feet,
And began to write a letter to his wife,
But lowered his head, instead, onto the table.

His heart trailed her nightgown on the floor.
He thought, In this house I have spent most of
My life. It's April. I am sixty-four,
And I have cancer . . . tries not to think, thinks of
His terror bayed in her deep white branches,
His breath vanishing in clouds white as her hair,
The floor's familiar stain, but he blanches
Seeing the stain, a dead man outlined there,
The house outliving him and all its dead.
It didn't matter anymore, but one
Could choose at last, could choose to hold his head,
Or stare into the mirror. Or use a gun.

Pages whisper, she turns to John: 16.
A moth beats small wings on the blank ceiling.
Her hand moves to her hair. The windows gleam.
Two years tonight. Outside, the stars keep shining.
Radiators knock, things rustle in the hedge.
She leans over her book, and there God leads
His animals to the purple water's edge
To die of thirst, she sees them as she reads,
Words left like bones along the river shore.
She turns the light out and the house is black.
She sits holding her book open, with no more
Thanks to give in prayer. Her fear comes back,
A bird, stripped to its bones, that cannot speak
For holding its own feathers in its beak.

3. ELIZABETH AND EBEN, 1940

He watered brick-bordered flower beds Saturday
And mowed and raked the lawn and weeded it,
Grass settling in his trouser cuffs and shoes.
She talked to him as she stood at the clothesline
Gathering his empty clothes into her arms,
Then swept, dusted, and baked, went shopping for
The Sunday dinner that they served today.
Their next-door neighbors came, their minister
Arrived promptly with flowers at one o'clock:
Lace tablecloth on gleaming mahogany,
Silver candlesticks, a bowl of polished fruit,
Pot roast with rich gravy, and mashed potatoes,
Applesauce, hot biscuits with raspberry jam,
Butter beans, ice water in cut-glass goblets,
The Chocolate Lovelight cake she's famous for,
And fresh hot coffee. The widower Johnson's
Square red face beneath white hair grew worried
That the pastor's wife might ask him what he thought
Of the sermon text her husband chose that day,
"Then said the trees unto the bramble, Come thou,
Reign over us," so he drew a breath
And offered his views of a town selectman:
"As for Williams, he's so broad he's flat."

The guests are gone. The dishes have been done.
They're in the living room, sitting within
The circle of the lamp. The evening steals
Over their windows, as over a pond.
Outside, June's tree toads peep; she talks
Softly, abstractedly running her hands

Over her stockings, straightening the seams.
His eyes darken looking at her amid
The sprays of rosebuds on their wallpaper,
The roses in their carpet. The hall clock whirs.
And on the small round table at her elbow
Their wedding photograph keeps under glass,
A young couple cutting their wedding cake.
Next to the photo sits a crystal bowl
Of water and white rocks where angelfish
Keep rising to a surface they can't break.

4. SUMMER EVENING

Footpaths shine in wet grass, the empty paths,
Black raspberries, apple scent, pears in the trees,
The roses' sleeping heads white on their leaves,
Small caterpillars slowly wave their horns.
Here little moves, but, like a swan, the moon
Riffles the surface, trails night in its wake.
On the lake's floor, this lawn, these trees,
These rooms, these lovers lie under a spell,
Lie in darkness and find the dark enough.
Indolent dusk, look down and envy me,
For I have married one with whom I'd lie
Until the vines grew up around our table,
Around our bed as if it were a tower
Guarding our sleep, where whistling birds alight,
Peace be within thy walls, prosperity
Within thy palaces—our walls and rooms
Enthralled by deep drugged vines and heart-shaped leaves
Where lovesick evening gathers, hangs, and grieves.

5 . ELIZABETH , 1905

Elizabeth bounces like a small white moth
Across the lawn, settling beneath a tree
To stitch her square of half-embroidered cloth,
Embroidering a house and family.
In blue and pink, words stream across the skies,
GOD BLESS OUR HOME. The movement of her eyes,
The motion of her arm pulling the thread.
She is one with the little girl she sewed.
Above her bent and concentrating head
The hundred-year-old pear tree's buds explode.

6. THE PICNIC, 1895

The photograph we found beneath the stair
Must have been dropped and left behind.
It shows our house, looming and white and square,
Late summertime.

A white horse grazes, three young women pose,
Their hats enormous, sleeves all lace
Blowing in small breezes that lift their clothes
Now here, now there, then chase

Their laughter, blow off things they've said
Like summer hats down hazy lanes.
Out through the open window overhead
Curtains billow like flames.

7 . THANKSGIVING DAY DOWNSTAIRS, 1858

Thanksgiving afternoon, and Charlotte waits
    On one foot, then the other,
    In the doorway: her mother
Eyes the great platters she decorates

With sugared grapes, while Cousin Jed debates
    With Pa, slavery and war.
    Through the buffet's glass door
The patterns painted on white dinner plates,

Blue willow trees, blue, half-hidden estates,
    Are delicate, and shine.
    She's old enough, at nine,
To set the table that accommodates

The tall uncles Pa sometimes imitates
    To make Ma laugh and scold.
    Charlotte needn't be told,
She knows, she'll whisper to her schoolmates

How each year Aunt Jerusha celebrates
    By drinking sherry
    And blushes red to see
Bachelor Moody, hat in hand, opening the gates.

8 . THANKSGIVING DAY UPSTAIRS,
1 8 5 8

Charles hears chairs scrape, familiar table prayers,
The clink of glass and silverware downstairs.
He watches patterns on the windows freeze.
Under the heavy blankets, his bent knees
Are mountain peaks, his feet volcanic isles,
The bed a thousand unexplored square miles
Of valleys, meadows—he balances on his lap
His precious atlas, opened to a map
Of North America. His frail, thin fingers
Hover over the continents, he lingers
Sea by sea, turning the wide blue pages.
He raids the coast, his men agree he wages
An astonishing campaign, sailing the covers
Beyond the book edges where he discovers
The white unbroken stretch of polar cold,
The green heat where the Holy Temple stands.
He looms over his maps, loving to hold
The wide world, like a story, in his hands.

But, dear blue boy, you gave a stone a name
One hundred years ago, and nothing came
To you except the footsteps like a promise,
Her hand upon your forehead, and the kiss
Familiar as the blankets you threw off
In sleep's red fever, and your burning cough,
Your dinner trays, your atlas, and your bed,
And secret tears for lives you would have led.

9 . THE LIVING ROOM

We've hung David's *La Vierge et les Saintes*
Near the piano. The companionable blessed
Surround the Virgin, her eyes are tolerant,
Dull with fulfillment. She is perfectly dressed,
Silk sleeves, green velvet gown, and jeweled cap;
Waves cascade down her back. Her Book of Hours,
Unlatched and lying open on her lap,
Reveals white, distant, miniature towers
Against a sky of pure, medieval blue,
Rude peasants worshipping, broad fields of wheat
Beneath the sun, moon, stars. A courtly zoo
Feeds in the letters, magnified, ornate,
The lion, monkey, fox, and snakes twining
Around the words amuse her. She chooses not
To read just now, but touches her wedding ring,
And round her waist a gold rope in a knot.
From where she sits, her eyes rest on the keys,
Watching my hands at practice. She enjoys
Bach in heaven, his sacred Fantasies
For her alone spin like fabulous toys.
Lines shift and break, she finds it rich and right,
Such music out of black dots on the page,
Symbols, the world a symbol from her height,
Great voices rising like smoke from time's wreckage.

Bach, like an epoch, at his clavichord,
Paused, listening, and shaking the great head
He watched his mind revolve. He pressed a chord.
He would compose tonight. Upstairs in bed
Anna Magdalyn worried, one o'clock

And him so tired, straining the clouded eyes to
Blindness; blindly for hours the master shook
The notes like legible blood drops onto
The page, Europe a small book in his palm,
Players in history's pages saying, "Not brook
But rather Ocean should be his name." At dawn
His wife awoke, the first on earth to hear
These silver lines beginning, plucked, revolved,
Unearthly trills spiraling up the stair,
The night dispelled, Leipzig itself dissolved,
And Paradise a figuring of air.

10. THE END OF THE WORLD, 1843

"And now the curtain shall be torn
And set on fire and tossed onto
The kindling sticks and rags of Earth:
Blow, Gabriel, to melt your horn!"
That year old women's rumors flew,
Harlots had given monsters birth,

Words in the clouds declared the hundred
Signs, locusts and toads, red skies
Like fire and blood; a fevered wind
Was heard to warn the mighty dead
To gather up their bones and rise;
Young girls saw flocks of angels in

The autumn trees, waiting. At night
Each girl sewed her Ascension Gown,
The women gathered at the well—
Their faces shone with wondrous light
Since William Miller came to town
And pitched a tent, preaching of Hell

With paper strips of published facts:
"Began B.C. 457,
Ends in 1843.
Children of God, your evil acts,
And evil thoughts, have angered Heaven!"
The townsfolk listened solemnly,

Went to the graveyard to await
On consecrated plots of ground

The horrible blast that would destroy,
Unspeakably, their low estate.
They waited for the furious sound
Week after week, until a boy

Impatiently climbed up on the roof
Of 19 Hadley Street and pressed
His tin horn to his lips and blew:
For Comfort Ferry it was proof
The world had ended, and he blessed
Himself before he swooned and grew

A nasty goose egg on his head;
And Esmerrianna Knott
Listened, then calmly bent to close
Her hem up with a gathering thread
So sinners left on earth could not
Look up her dress as she arose.

11. HALLOWEEN

The children's room glows radiantly by
The light of pumpkins on the windowsill
That fiercely grin on sleeping boy and girl.
She stirs and mutters in her sleep, Goodbye,

Who scared herself a little in a sheet
And walked the streets with devils and dinosaurs
And bleeping green men flown from distant stars.
We sit up late, and smoke, and talk about

Our awkward, loving Frankenstein in bed
Who told his sister that it isn't true,
That real men in real boxes never do
Haunt houses. But the King of the Dead

Has taken off his mask tonight, and twirled
His cape and vanished, and we are his
Who know beyond all doubt how real he is:
Out of his bag of sweets he plucks the world.

12. SAMUEL JUDD, 1820

You didn't know your date of birth, you said;
Some swore that you were older than the flood.
You'd bare discolored teeth, shaking your head,
And curse like summer thunder, Samuel Judd.

Still, to see you toiling down the stair,
Or standing crooked at your crooked door,
Or on the front porch in your rocking chair,
One wouldn't know that you were hard at war:

You tied tin cans on strings for your alarms.
You'd doze, the Good Book sliding from your knees,
And at a sound you'd jump, flapping your arms
To scare off children from your apple trees.

13. THE PAPERWEIGHT

The scene within the paperweight is calm,
A small white house, a laughing man and wife,
Deep snow. I turn it over in my palm
And watch it snowing in another life,

Another world, and from this scene learn what
It is to stand apart: she serves him tea
Once and forever, dressed from head to foot
As she is always dressed. In this toy, history

Sifts down through the glass like snow, and we
Wonder if her single deed tells much
Or little of the way she loves, and whether he
Sees shadows in the sky. Beyond our touch,

Beyond our lives, they laugh, and drink their tea.
We look at them just as the winter night
With its vast empty spaces bends to see
Our isolated little world of light,

Covered with snow, and snow in clouds above it,
And drifts and swirls too deep to understand.
Still, I must try to think a little of it,
With so much winter in my head and hand.

14. THE PARSONAGE, 1785

Reverend Eliphet Swift, man of the Lord,
Your parish crowded our front rooms, parlors, halls,
For wakes and weddings. Your letters record
So many shad swarming South Hadley Falls
That as you rowed you struck them with your oars.
You put St. Andrew's cross above each latch
To scare away the witches from your doors,
And from these windows you would stand and watch
Storms break on good and bad, your penitents
Like boulders in the field. You were a rock:
No painted likeness, books, or instruments,
No silver spoons, no mirror, and no clock,
No Salem glassware, no excessive light
From candelabra—let the woman fuss.
Enough for you to have a fire each night,
And spring each year rose green as Lazarus.

Eliphet Swift, you knew why you came West,
Stranding your sisters on the village shores
To Bibles and rising bread, ten, twelve times blest
With child, your mother anxious at her chores,
Your father gone to sea, and in your stead
Your brother after him, and then the whale
That smashed his ship, leaving your brother dead.
You kept seeing Leviathan's great tail
Parting the sea like God, black noise, black air.
One hundred miles inland: still you could smell
Fear churning like an ocean in your prayer.
Christ knew the water, chose to row through hell.

You watched the empty shells, rinsed in the tide
—And fled. But crucifixes on your walls
Were hulks of whale hanging from His Ship's side.
Your last years found you fishing at the Falls.

15. THE MEETING IN THE KITCHEN, 1740

Scissors, tallow, sieve, and knife,
Balls of twine and weather vanes,
Meadows filled with spadefoot frogs,
Says Cotton Witt has took to wife
A witch, and her alone explains
Our frost of June, our rabid dogs,

Our sickles broke, our oxen drowned.
Spiddy Preston took to bed
With bee stings blistering both her arms
After she chased Witt's pigs around
Her flax garden, and now she's dead.

Lord keep the Devil from our farms.

The future opens like a grave
Unless our incantation save
South Hadley from this witch's bite,
Star of Wormwood, Tree of Night.

16. EBENEZER MARSH, 1725

Your windows were the biggest in the town,
Your walls were papered, pillows filled with down
On great four-posters under family portraits,
The shelves laden with tamarinds, sweetmeats,
Hyson, Bohea, Congo, and green teas,
Citrons and lemons from the West Indies—
But still you saw, beyond your orchard wall,

The exiles and executions, and the squall
Of Bloody Mary digging up the dead,
England convulsed, and the Protestant head
Of your great-great-grandfather in a pail
For claiming that the Pope concealed a tail
Beneath his glittering robes, the ship of strangers
Sailing to the world's end, and the dangers
Of your boyhood, haunting your settlement.
Lately the savage, shrunk into his tent

Near the Quonektakut, subdued and meek,
Idle, thriftless, seemed to forget that week
Of beating drums, when even praying Indians
Connived to sell for English knives and guns
White children. Your mother lost her wits
When news came that a squaw was torn to bits
By village dogs in Hockanum. She dreamed
Chief Quonquont waved his arms and screamed:
You knew that scream was war, was war, was war,

Like an axe buried in a wooden door
That scream was driven hard into your brain,

The bright red skies, the burning grain
And stolen stock, the stink and smoking waste
Of Springfield sacked and burned. The taste, the taste
Of ashes on your lips would not subside:
Thou shalt eat and not be satisfied.

Nor satisfied with wealth in your old age,
Your apple orchard, your richly blessed marriage,
Your generous entertainments. And of all
You owned, only the house is left. We call
It ours, the rooms, the cry within the stair,
The carved face stricken on the banister.
Outside, the tree they say you planted turns
Its leaves to hell-of-flames and silent burns,
Clenching its fist of roots around the earth,
For all a fistful of garden dirt is worth.
It shades the house, shades the abandoned garden,
Like an overwhelming need for pardon.

THE

LAMPLIT

ANSWER

(1985)

☼

FOR MY SISTERS
ANN, MARY, AND DIKKA

I

KREMLIN OF SMOKE

Chopin in the Faubourg Saint-Germain. Winter 1831

1. The Salon

The swan's neck of the teacup, her black vizard
Plunged underwing, conceals her face like a modest cocotte
Who can't bring herself to look up at the honored guest,
As the silver hammer of the tea service practices
Chings in runs of triplets, and the tea steam hangs
Phantom chrysanthemums on long, evaporating stems
In the air of the winter apartment. The guests,
Having gathered for games, for mimicries,
For gossip's intricate, expensive inventions,
Crowd toward the pianist who, leaning forward,
Clasps his hands, like a child's prison for butterflies,
To begin a tale, perfected in his room, of his
Reception on a tour in the South, where they had hired
A sedan chair with servants to bear him to the theater,
"Like a captured king from a remote, Saxon metropolis,"
And then killed him in the reviews—a smashing joke,
And his hostess snaps her fan shut when she laughs,
In the city of slaves to mirrors, of rivalries
Championed for less than a day by charlatans,
Of politics lending heat to the rented rooms
Of exiled virtuosos, and of cholera warnings affixed
To the posts of the streetlamps, whose heads
Flare with fever from here to the outermost districts.

2. Warsaw, 1820

The year of childhood's sickbed strewn with novels,
His mother being addicted to the romances
Of Rousseau, although she called them packs of lies,
When four o'clock's dim lamps beatified
With crimson gilt the borders of the pears
And crescent cakes she brought to usher in
The time she set aside to waste with him
In blissful episodes of idle talk,
Each day, during his fortnight's influenza,
They shuffled cards in slow-collapsing bridges,
And dealt out suits like secret city factions
Whose spreading fans could hide conspiracies
For dealing heavy blows to czars at teatime.
And once, the household clocks passing the news
Of "Five" from room to room, when she stood up
To put away the cards and cold tea,
He, wishing he could keep her there with him,
Thought to detain her with interrogations
And, sinking back to watch the rushing heights
Of falling snow beyond the window glass,
Began by asking her, Where is the snow from?

And overarching the cream cakes, the pale-skinned meringues,
And the candied violets arranged among the bibelots of the old
Legitimist Bourbons, the pipes and cigars of bespectacled
Millionaire guests fling a kremlin of smoke overhead,
Dome upon dome, rising up to the mauve-tinted heaven
Of trompe-l'oeil clouds, as Chopin, stolen from
The *Comédie* by the piano gods, with a tablecloth over
His shoulders, enacts "My Viennese Laundress." He points
To the imaginary trays of the French sausagemaker's
Shop-window display, and quavers in an indignant contralto,
"Ach! Those sausages were ground from dogs und alley cats,
Mein Herr, und the remains of guillotined aristocrats!"
Dome upon dome, from which orders issue to plunder
His childhood home, while here the hostess lifts her hand,
At which high-sign the grand piano is rolled in,
Its curving wing unfolded, like a great black butterfly
That slowly sails toward charades by candlelight
Across the polished chasm of parquet.

He thought she hadn't heard him, seeing how
She stopped, as if enchanted, hands outstretched
And frozen half in flight above the cards,
Her profile turned three-quarters toward the glass,
A statue stolen from last summer's game
Of Statues, when his great-aunt's hand composed
The winning title for his mother's pose
As "Time, caught in the act of listening
Outside the walls of music." Then he heard it,
The dreaded, spectral carriages of thunder
Rolling toward their house, like the Grand Duke
—Pavlovich!—coming to fetch the prodigy
In an amusing, minor act of war:
Subjection in the form of flattery
Heaped on the Polish people's little star
Scavenged from Warsaw's cultural debris,
A star still at the age whose wishbones bleach,
Forgotten, in the dining-room armoire,
The age of funerals held for nightingales.
But then, when she resumed her task again,
She answered neither, What? nor, I don't know.
Rather, turning her profile from the glass
That cut in half a slowly building drift
Like the cross-section of an empty palace,
She answered him, The snow—it comes from Moscow.

His irritation at the threshold's creak
Beneath the servant's foot this afternoon
Had seemed rather enacted than experienced,
His petulant rebuke, the spectacle
In which it seemed he played it to the hilt,
An exiled Master flown into a passion
Who'd fled a nine-year-old's piano lesson
To lock himself upstairs into his room.
And while his scolded pupil's lowered face
In silhouette above the keyboard wore
His reprimand in prisms on her lashes,
A sylph staring, up close, into a pearl—
The glamour of vain outbursts lost on her,
The sweeping gesture of his obstinate
Refusal, even now, to come downstairs!—
A tantrum nearly comical, except
His struggle to restrain his brimming tears
And effort to choke back his wish to blame
Her threw him back onto his couch
Forceful as if self-pity could foreguess
How, from the fourth-floor window of a house
In Warsaw occupied by Russian soldiers,
The soldiers on a lark have seized and hurled,
As if thunder itself turned visible,
Chopin's piano crashing to the street,
And burned the wreck—though here in fact,
Surrounded by the yards of silk he's hung

Around his room "gray as the river Seine,"
He doesn't know for what it is he cries;
And holds, swimming before his eyes, no image
But his pair of slippers through a heavy blur,
Embroidered slippers propped and motionless,
And, pictured in the blind-stitched calla lily's
White, upwhirling spathe, a burning bridge.

Bayed in the lap of the Marchioness, the littlest
And most charming monkey in Paris, who appears
To have crossed childhood's threshold middle-aged,
Murders a lily, wringing it by the stem,
Then flings it aside as the recital begins,
And the powder shaken from the lily's horn
Scatters like crumbs of fire across the floor,
As a Nocturne, circling the room, floats out
Above the sidewalks of the faubourg among
The snowbound lanterns, whose dimmed flames
Smolder behind their framed, white squares of snow
That verge on disintegration—as a page,
Ignited on the grate and now gone cold,
Maintains its structure as a work of ash
Whose letters breathe like ghosts of butterflies
Barely respiring, and legible unless
Gloved fingertips should touch them curiously
And make them crumble: "You are a Russian, God!"
Upstairs, applause breaks out like muffled war,
And on the street a dozen men have ceased
To knock the heaps of snow to fragile flocks,
But fling aside their shovels to applaud.

7. Warsaw, 1822

There the beloved pelican, dressed in a shredded frock coat,
With a purplish nose and the lavender, lopsided wig
Got at a steal from King Stanislav's auctioned-off wardrobe,
Would, mid-lesson, the better to emphasize his points,
Arise into a carpet-slipper quadrille and wave
His stick in lightning shapes before the boy
Already proclaimed the Russian nobles' darling,
Admonishing: Now! Thunder away like mad! Think big!
The professor who, at the close of their final lesson,
Had counted off on his once-famous fingers
The five things every pianist must remember:

One, to ignore the unthinkable folly of Weber;
Two, to ignore every so-called Italian composer;
Three, to ignore the conventions surrounding one's need
For a bath, since a rubdown with vodka will do;
Four, to ignore Ludwig Beethoven—too cataclysmic;
Five, most important, this last being saved for the thumb,
To ignore where you are and whomever it is you perform for:
"Larks, for example—what do they care who deposes
The King of all Poland? I needn't say I refer
To the Viceroy, may he and his uncles and aunts
And his furthest descendants, however remote, burn
Forever—but the larks will give tongue to a phrase
Neither Polish nor Russian, and do so as freely
From the branches of trees in the private park
Of the archfiend as in your mother's kitchen-garden, son.

And what are their motives for singing?"—turning his hand
Slowly over to empty out nothing—"Precisely none."

8. Chopin's Journal

September 1831. The Fall of Warsaw

Once I have grasped it, a fever comes out
Hanging lanterns on the wide staircases,
One by one, leading to the courtyard where,
Though I advocate nothing, still my eyes
Detect within the eyes of my companion
The imperceptible paranoia of the charlatan,
Like hummingbirds taking sugar-water sips,
Flickering scarlet tints in his irises.
So the topic is flowers, and proposing to contemplate
Their aristocratic deaths, I say, "In Poland
We say the crown is reached only through
The imagination," as from a silver tray
Of showy blossoms I choose one to twirl
By its stem: a creamy camellia, ruffled
As the hem of the Marquise's gown, through which
The maid's heavy iron slowly drifted
That she may longer twirl and twirl beneath
The arbor where lilacs foam along
The crest of the waltz craze, though the first
Mottles of corruption edge the petals,
Like the tarnish on the scissors which
Decapitated it. Flowers, because
I too am an outcome withering from my cause.

THE SELF-PORTRAIT OF
IVAN GENERALIĆ

The school of naïve painters, Hlebine, Yugoslavia. Oil on glass, 1975

Once distant villages hung in the trees
Like God the Father's stars, and pigs transformed
The grass with wedding feasts, and goslings swarmed

Running like kindergarteners from the geese,
Glad in the farmyards of the sacred heart,
The windows of the Lord where sunsets brimmed

Around the heads of sheep, as gold-leaf rimmed
The gospel pages where we played a part
Until God chased you crying from the world:

There we were saved. Lambs stepped on skinny legs
To baby-sit the hidden, fragile eggs
When birds, flown to the Crucifixion, swirled

And snapped the fresh white linen in their beaks,
Draping the shroud of Jesus in the yard.
But now I take it back, I take it hard,

I take it up with Him whose evening streaks
The violet flash of Christ beyond the fence,
As tears make purple clouds of Bible ink

On gospel leaves of onionskin. I think
Of roots touching your face in ignorance.
Once onions curled like gospels from your knife,

Once roosters spread their wings like Christ entombed
But risen, stepping through the stony room
The way foals rise and wobble into life

Before their mothers' eyes. I take it back.
Instead our windows darken into squares
Of night, from which you've vanished, window squares

Like Bibles closed forever, squares of black.

SIGNS

Threading the palm, a web of little lines
Spells out the lost money, the heart, the head,
The wagging tongues, the sudden deaths, in signs
We would smooth out, like imprints on a bed,

In signs that can't be helped, geese heading south,
In signs read anxiously, like breath that clouds
A mirror held to a barely open mouth,
Like telegrams, the gathering of crowds—

The plane's X in the sky, spelling disaster:
Before the whistle and hit, a tracer flare;
Before rubble, a hairline crack in plaster
And a housefly's panicked scribbling on the air.

TWO TALES OF CLUMSY

1

When Clumsy harks the gladsome ting-a-lings
Of dinner chimes that Mrs. Clumsy rings,
His two hands winglike at his most bald head,
Then Clumsy readies Clumsy to be fed.
He pulls from satchel huge a tiny chair,
And waggling his pillowed derriere

He hitches up his pants to gently sit.
Like two ecstatic doves his white hands flit
Tucking his bib in quickly, then, all thumbs,
They brush away imaginary crumbs
From knee-high table with dismissive air.
With fists wrapped round his giant silverware

He shuts his eyes and puckers up for kisses.
In such a pose Clumsy awaits his Mrs.,
Rubbing his hungry ribs. But oh, alack,
Quite unbeknownst to Clumsy, at his back
The circle of a second spotlight shows
That No-No has delivered fatal blows

To Mrs. Clumsy since that happy time
She summoned Clumsy with her dinner chime.
And there is Clumsy's darling lying dead.
How like a rubber ball bounces her head
As No-No drags her feet-first from this life.
Then No-No dresses up as Clumsy's wife,

Her scarf now silhouettes his long hooked nose,
His long bones rattle in her frilly clothes
As No-No brings a tray of cups and plates
Into the light where puckered Clumsy waits.
Hearing her footstep soft makes Clumsy take
The pucker from his lips and sweetly break

Into falsetto greetings, then resume
His lips into a kiss. But this is doom,
And hideously silent No-No stands.
When Clumsy parts his eyelids both his hands
Fly up as if on strings and Clumsy screams,
The tears squirt from his ducts a dozen streams,

His mouth blubbers, inelegantly smeared,
"Where is she, No-No? Oh, I am afeared!"
Then No-No lifts up Clumsy's trembly chin,
And leans to hiss with loud stage whisper in
The big pink ear of Clumsy, "My dear friend,"
No-No enunciates. "This is The End."

2

Disguised as Doctor of Philosophy
In academic haberdashery
By dint of hood and black capacious gown,
No-No wipes off the blackboard up and down,
His black sleeve floating outward with each lunge,
The black streaks glisten from his dampened sponge,

While Clumsy sharpens pencils two feet long
To little stubs and wets them with his tongue,
Then smooths his pad of paper with gloved fists.
He lifts his sleeves a fraction at the wrists
And twirls his hands around like windmill sails
To soothe his nerves, then drums his muffled nails

Until the Doctor claps his hands rat-tat
And picks his pointer up and points it at
His eager pupil with the jumbo ears:
"Compose a paragraph." And Clumsy clears
His throat a dozen times to soft aver,
"I don't know how to write with letters sir."

At which the Doctor hides with sleeve a smile
Most uncontrollable and fraught with guile,
Until, authority regained, he says,
"In that case you may dictate sentences
Which you most wish to write, and I'll record
Your words for you to copy from the board."

Now Clumsy tries to think of what to write.
He cranes his neck around stage-left and -right,
He gazes toward the rafters thinking hard
And sometimes shakes his head as to discard
Ideas he finds less than adequate,
Then caroling a joyous "I know what!"

He pulls a giant lightbulb from a sack
And holds it overhead and puts it back,
And in his vast excitement both his hands
Pull up his earlobe-anchored rubber bands
To lift from scalp his tiny frizzy wig:
"I'd like to start with 'God is very big.'"

Erupting laughter nearly knocks quite down
The Doctor in his nearly empty gown,
He whirls on heel and cuts his hooting off:
"My theologian! Fellow *philosophe*!
Your disquisition has the resonance
Of truth's unique, unutterable sense

But yet, being pedantic and antique,
This mind of mine must tinker, weigh, and seek,
And wonder if together you and I
For sake of scholarship should specify
How big God is?" Thus groping for the truth
About the size of God makes pink smoke poof

From Clumsy's ears in jets, and fire alarms
Go off backstage as, lowered head on arms,
Full sixty seconds Clumsy cogitates.
The Doctor snaps his chalk in two and waits.
Clumsy looks up and No-No utters "Yes?"
"Bigger than the biggest clouds, I guess."

"Bigger than clouds! Dear fellow! I should say
I never would have thought of God that way!
Then let's begin." And No-No sets the chalk
Tick-ticking on the board like time-bomb clock
While Clumsy wraps his pencil finger-wise
And sets it on the page and squints his eyes

At No-No's blackboard words so white and clean
And neat and straight with spaces in between,
And then, his page two inches from his nose,
He copies out in crooked uphill rows:
"I, Clumsy, hereby give and wittingly
My soul to No-No for Eternity."

II

IMAGINARY PRISONS

A version of "Sleeping Beauty." In memory of Colin Way Reid

The gardeners gazing through their open shears
Or staring sightless from their wooden ladders
Stand helpless by and dream they cannot lower

Their upraised sickles poised a hundred years
Above the labyrinth of stems, as briars,
Even while dreaming of their destinies

As smoke and ashes in the gardeners' fires,
Fasten themselves around the spellbound blades
And steal the dreamers' hats in mockery

To lift them out of reach of stick and ladder,
Then lose them on their way to taking over
The twilit walls and roofs and hundred chimneys

Against whose edifices chimney swallows
Have woven for their families habitations
With rosebud twigs and dust of crumbled mortar

And threads they've tugged gently as milliners
From out the silken shirts and ruffled trousers
Of failed princes hidden in the brambles,

The swallows unaware these men have starved
Entangled in their struggles with the briars.
Yet every year more numerous and scary

These faces one by one among the roses
Bear witness to the private agony
Of what it means to have a single purpose.

Peacocks patrol the garden's sleeping borders
Malicious as a troop of evil fairies
Who pace and lash the brickwork with their feathers'

Opalescent hems, and pacing screech
How perilous is purity of heart.
And briars tentatively hoist their thorns

Across the dizzying ledges schisms form
Where being and non-being break apart.

*

The kitchen boy distracted by a quarrel
Is dreaming that he opens up a box
Of banished knives blinding even at twilight

And this way makes his adversary cower,
But ducks in fact before the furnace-stoker
Around whose lifted shovel embers sparkle

And hang like bumblebees around a flower.
And though you laugh, to them it greatly matters,
For they've had confirmation of the rumor

Touching upon the kitchen maid's betrothal;
The girl whom both of them have tried to capture
Like awkward brooms chasing a wind-borne feather

Today revealed her secret plans to marry
A woodcutter from the adjoining forest
Who's older than both rivals put together,

The only man the girl has wanted ever.
But tell me, seeing how in joy her fingers
Touch her reflection in the plate of copper

It is her task to breathe upon and burnish
As gently as a sleeper barely breathing,
Say who could wish the future on another?

For she must wake from momentary rapture
Into a grief approaching lunacy
To learn, among the skeletons of princes,

A humbler man has long since lost the struggle
And witnessed to the end the work of briars
As, blooming through his slowly loosened fingers,

They carried off his ax as if it were
A weightless toy among the waves of roses.
Upstairs her mistress in a sitting chamber

Has drawn a diamond from a velvet sack
Intending to bequeath it to her daughter,
But transfixed in the dream with palm outstretched

As though to weigh a flame she seems to shiver
In finding that the diamond, howsoever
Its light wobbles unstable as a fire,

Feels to her sightless fingers icy black.

*

The mountain ranges on the moon never
So near as now, never so clear, never
So brilliant with a brimming tenderness

As here before the court astronomer
Who sleeps beguiled at his telescope
And dreams he has beheld the final vision,

Granted after the lifetime he has given
To studying the systems of the night.
He dreams, sunk in a lit, celestial slumber,

That lifting up his eyes he has observed
Beyond the black of night the boundary
And inner surface of the crystal sphere

And curved foundation wall of the sublime
By which we are enclosed, he dreams, with light,
Where black to rushing radiance is transformed

And matter into spirit evanesced.
He dreams his life's not wasted, furthermore,
For all is as his formulas suggest,

The diagrams and models of the worlds
Which he's spent years committing to the care
Of tranquil, pencil-covered papers rest

All in perfect accord with what he sees.
So let him sleep, and sleep enthralled, and never
Mind that it's a false discovery,

And please, don't pipe up that the obstacle
Of blackness which he dreams he's looking through
Is just as black as it was black before,

And fully insurmountable as ever.
For you and I know walls as high or higher,
And each of us has dreamed a private terror,

Or call it whatsoever you desire,
Disintegrates and blows away and clears
Our paths until we waken to discover

The very thing we thought had disappeared
Still waits for us in silence up ahead.
So leave him his perfected universe

Fulfilled as it was promised in his theory,
Leave him the page on which his calipers
Are perched and shining like a triangle

Of light beams springing from his pencil marks.
Leave him, though you and I are taught the sky
Is backed up by a blackness like a hammer

Already fallen on his circular
Irradiated dream as if the spheres
Were balls of glass shattered in jagged angles

Even geometry is dumbstruck by.

*

The seamstress caught up in a dream of sewing
Is dreaming that in lieu of banished scissors
She can't employ to cut an abstract pattern

She can't affix to cloth with banished pins,
Is dreaming that her two hands grip a flowing
Bolt of cloudy, lightning-colored fabric

Which she is poised with all her rapt attention
To tear in one electric flash of noise.
And clowning like a slave of comedy

The aging simpleton whom she has hired
In sympathy is pressing in his fervor
The bonnet top which he elects to wear

To keep the weather off winter and summer,
And dreaming of his job of chasing flies.
Beneath the shadow of his lifted swatter,

The housefly dreams she wrings her hands with worry.
Below this workshop lies the court's despairing
Lone perpetual insomniac,

Alarmed as if he overheard their dreaming.
But seeing how he's grown perversely eager,
Lying flat out and hopeless on his back,

To learn at last which sound will finally shatter
His nerves so thoroughly that it will keep
His body, mind, and soul awake forever,

I'll grant you that it's something of a challenge
To stifle giggles, for, with sheets and covers
Pulled up around his wakeful head adorned

With layered nightcaps like a crown of flannel
With puffy parts for muffling the ears,
He looks like some unheard-of king of cabbage

Condemned forever in his lonely garden
To dreaming that he cannot fall asleep.

*

Assigned to live next door, because he's silent,
Though under lock and key, because he's mad,
The ruler's brother sits with elbows propped

And hands holding his face above the trestle,
Regarding through the prison of his fingers
The specter of an empty china platter

As he's regarded it for countless years
Since he was thunderstricken to discover
A trivial flaw disastrous to his theory

In which the world is made of porcelain,
But porcelain that cannot crack or shatter
As demonstrated in his published paper,

"The Paradigm of Glass Unbreakable,"
With which he thought to rectify the anger
Of those like him who'd keenly felt the bitter

Accident of being dropped and broken.
And yet the dunderheads refused to hear!
And given that the blind, refining forces

Which glaze the world in an ideal fire
Appeared to have no meaning to the others,
He ceased evangelizing and retired,

Dropping exhausted to his study chair,
And turned to meditation to restore
His faith and to refresh his memory

By summoning the specter of a platter
To represent our wholly perfect order,
And that's the moment, as I said before,

That this unfortunate was struck by thunder
And terrified to see, and no mistaking,
The surface showed the first hint of a fissure,

A web of cracks across the porcelain
Like black lightning unrolled and fixed forever
Into the lightly shattered glaze was creeping,

A test of faith which lengthened year by year
Before his swearing of a vow to stare
Until the fragile web of laws breaking

The tragic glaze apart come to appear
To be the laws by which it's held together.

*

Behind the man trapped in the labyrinths
And mazes of his theory's shattered beauty,
The chimney sweep like an incongruous

And homely soldier standing at attention
Is troubled into a dream of reverence
Since he in the fulfillment of his duty

With savage mop widowed a chimney swallow
Whose voice, he dreams, still flutes from out-of-doors
Like a petition for the simplest mercy,

Calling his mate back from a territory
No mapmaker is hired to consider,
One prison engineered within another

And hidden in the blackness of the chimney.
Though you and I are schooled in the motto
That goes, "A stranger's tears are only water,"

Though we hold in the very least regard
The sentiments of such a worthless rascal
As does to death an ordinary swallow,

And though you scoff that having murdered her
The boy is stunned before her crumpled figure,
That he once having seen the swallow fallen,

And with a premonition of disaster,
Is moved to doff his cap and mourn in honor
Of one however small who has crossed over

The line dividing nothingness from history,
If you think "nothingness" goes way too far,
If "history" is the word that sets you crowing

It isn't history if it isn't written—
It's written here, and written here in memory
Of one who's flown ahead of us to enter

That nothing than which there is nothing vaster.

*

The angelfish streaming their whispered letters
Are dreaming they turn back from what they whisper
To flee along their unseen, drifting ladders,

Abandoned in the poet's empty quarters
Since he was carted off a prisoner
And charged, lacking the benefit of lawyers,

With sharpening his pencil to a point
Nearly approaching the invisible.
Absurd, you say, that any could consider

A pencil point a real and present danger,
Yet here he keeps, in the remotest tower,
The company of sundry malefactors

All dressed in jailbird hats and jailbird shirts,
And dreams his angelfish are drawing near
The paper he's spread out across his table,

Like candle flames they flicker as they whisper
The letters he transcribes, and back and forth
Their wobbling reflections through the water

Give to the page an underlight of fire
As if fire were a property of paper.
And drowsing next to him, the king's birdkeeper,

Arrested for importing foreign birds
Sharp-beaked enough to constitute a peril,
Is dreaming that the brass keys of the jailer

Chirp in the locks of manacles and fetters,
Soft as the first in all the aviary
To voice a note before the blackness clears.

Nearby the drunkard dreams of foaming beer,
The counterfeiter dreams of flawless money
That issues from his confiscated needle

In spectral temples, webs, and ghostly scrolls
Blooming in portraitures of shadowed numerals.
Nearby the painter, dragged in by the collar

For spending his allotment for a year's
Supply of paints on one half ounce of umber,
Is dreaming that his new-laid patch of plaster

Is parching dry as desert sand before
He's able to complete his fragmentary
Fresco of utopian waterways

Where dolphin-leaps like transitory doors
To palaces across the water form
Shining parabolas above canals.

*

Here too, wrongly denounced as a false servant
When he foresaw the devastating scandal
Attendant on the infant's christening,

And then arrested on the ruler's orders
When he described the blackness furthermore
Which Beauty at the hour of betrayal

Would see within the light of birthday candles,
The court's clairvoyant dreams that on the stairs
That spiral downward to his darkened parlor

His wife is standing stricken at the door,
Reading the posted writ of his arrest
As if the black-gloved hand of the informer

Were laid directly on her narrow shoulder.
And you and I can see: his dream is true.
Nodding above his handcuffs in the corner,

And exiled from all company, but for
The presence of two mirror-image spiders
Who dream they wage an obscure tournament,

The traitor dreams of climbing up a ladder
Reaching from prison moat to prison tower,
Although a tower less and less familiar,

And dreams, casting his eyes over his shoulder,
He sees the ladder upside down in water,
Himself as he climbs higher growing smaller,

Himself as he looks downward looking upward,
And dreams he scrambles, falls, and crashes toward
His death with outstretched arms, and there

Is met by no one but the water's mirrored
Looming, panicked image of himself.

*

The king's uneasiness at coming trauma
Compels him to the shop of the clockmaker
Where one by one on his more desperate orders

According to his right of search-and-seizure
The kingdom's clocks were hauled in all together
And all of them, like world-is-ending seers

Incarcerated for the way they chatter,
Telling obsessively a single story
Over and over, all reduced the ruler

To telling them, Shut up! Shut up! Shut up!
And now dismantled, emptied, strewn in parts
Across the benches, tables, sills, and floors,

They've fallen silent as their very maker
Who sits with his demolished masterworks
And following instructions slowly lowers

His brush dejected into paint dissolver
To swab away the black of painted numbers
From every clock face in the territory,

The disassembled royal water-chimes,
The cuckoo clocks wearing a look of terror,
The grandfathers dumped out like ransacked drawers,

The microcosmic wheels and golden gears
And useless screws and labyrinths of wires
And miniature bells and gongs and hammers

And swaying springs like just-beheaded roses
And black unfastened dials pointing where
There's nothing left to point at but the ruler

Who with his crown exchanged for the watchmaker's
Headband with the lens extended forward
Is breathless with attention bending over

The timepiece of his father's father's father
Which he is touching with the jeweler's
Diminutive, unaging pair of tweezers

As if to halt once and for all the source
Of seconds, minutes, hours, days, and years.
And this is how we find him, as he stares

Sightless into the ruined factory
Bequeathed to him, and dreams that he discovers
The future isn't manufactured there—

It's manufactured somewhere in the past,
The present in the past, past in the past,
It lies beyond his legislative power

Though banging gavels bring his courts to order
And pound out points of law as sharp or sharper
Than pencils, pins and needles, knives and scissors:

The future in the past is fixed forever,
Like words locked up in pencils, webs in spiders,
Like flames imprisoned in the match tip's sulphur,

Like thorns locked up in seeds hidden in roses
Imprisoned in the budding stems of briars.
He cannot overrule the condemnation:

More patient than a needle in a drawer,
It is the past that lies in wait for her,
Concealing in a point grown ever sharper

The blood drops of the mock assassination—

*

And rightly dreams he cannot save another.
And though you rush to say he rests assured
Of the compassion of the dispensation,

And though the promised torch already burns
By which the briars are lit and roses turn
To smoke and ashes in the gardeners' fires

Through which the true prince walks and is unharmed,
I've learned to make a study of the hour
When grander schemes that mock our calculations

Reveal that we're the emblems standing for
The consequence of what we cannot master.
Say what you wish about the past and future,

But we have learned that here and now is where
All time stops in a face we've held as dear
As she is held who's overcome with roses,

And now is never where the promised fires
Are burning, but the time that's set apart
For you and I to stand and sightless stare,

As gardeners gazing through their open shears
Stand in the shadows of the promised briars.

III

☀

COMPLAINT

I lean over the rail toward the dark town,
The rail a streak of cloud in piled snow,
The stairs cloud-piled around the balcony.
His house is lit below,

One light among the branches at my feet.
I look, and press my hands into the snow.
I think that I am inconsolable.
No path to him, I know

Of none but that I follow into sleep
To where he waits, I hurry through the snow
To where the man stands waiting in the dream.
He loves, he tells me so,

He kisses me until the ceiling dome
Parts overhead and snow is coming through,
Until heaven itself, empty of snow,
Opens above us too,

His hands melting the snow into my hair
Until I wake. Since he'll not have me, no,
I come out to the balcony and press
My hands into the snow,

And close my eyes, since he is blind to me.
Since he'll not hear me, then I'll be deaf too,
And draw my hair into a set of strings
I'll take a scissors to.

SONATA

Overture

More loudly to inveigh against your absence,
Raising the volume by at least a third,
Humbly I say I've written this immense
Astonishing "Sonata" word by word,
With leitmotivs you'll wish you'd never heard,
And a demented, shattering Cadenza.
I'm pained to say that scholarship insists
Cadenzas are conclusion to Concertos,
Not Sonatas—true Sonatas close
With what pedantic musicologists,
Waving their Ph.D.s beneath my nose,
Persist in calling Recapitulation.
My double ending is a Variation:
I couldn't choose between them once I chose
To write two endings, so, because I wrote a
Recapitulation and Cadenza,
My piece concludes two times—and then it ends
Again because I've added on a Coda.

To brush up on Sonata structure: first,
The Exposition sounds two melodies,
Deeply dissimilar, in different keys,
Major and minor. Part Two is a burst
Of brainstorms scholars call Development,
In which the two themes of the Exposition
Are changed and rearranged past recognition,
Distorted, fragmented, dissolved, and blent

Into chromatic superimposition,
Till, imperceptibly, two themes unite.
And then, if everything is going right,
The piece concludes in Recapitulation.

Exposition

Theme One: My life lacks what, in lacking you?
Theme Two: Does the material world exist?

(Ideally your neurons should resist,
As yet, connecting Numbers One and Two.
But note the skill, the frightening mastery,
The lunatic precision it entails
To merge these separate themes, the way train rails
Converge as they approach infinity.)

I dreamed that an encyclopedia
Opened before my eyes and there I found
Analogies to sort of stack around
My what-is-life-without-you-here idea:

Like *nous* detached from Anaxagoras,
Like cosmic fire glimmering without
A Heraclitus there to find it out,
Like square roots waiting for Pythagoras,
Like One-ness riven from Parmenides,
Like Nothing without Gorgias to detect it,
Like paradox sans Zeno to perfect it,
Like plural worlds lacking Empedocles,
Like Plato's chairs and tables if you took
The furniture's Eternal Forms away,
Objects abandoned by Reality
Still look the same, but look the way things look
When I behold my life without you in it:
A screwy room where chairs and tables lack
Dimension from the front, the side, the back,
Like finity without the infinite,
Where tea parties are held without the Hatter,
It's like a single point withdrawn from Space,
It's like a physicist who cannot trace
The ultimate constituents of matter—

There is no evidence Matter exists.
Thus do I introduce Theme Number Two.
And I can't prove it, but I know it's true:
The physical eludes the physicists.
They've chased down matter past atomic rings
Into small shadows, and they've lost it there.
It seems that they can't find it anywhere.
They stalk imaginary floating things
Like amateurish lepidopterists
Round babbling brooks and mossy fairy knolls.
Their net strings map out squares of empty holes.
Behold them snatching something in their fists:
Their fingers uncurl, cautious, on the sight
Of Nothing crushed against the sweaty hand.
But then I'm prejudiced, you understand.
Not everyone on earth believes I'm right.
But lest you think I'm kidding, or perverse,
I went to hear a Lecture just last year
About some things which I hold very dear:
The smallest pieces of the universe.
The Lecturer referred to them as Quarks.
He seemed impervious to the mystery
Surrounding their invisibility.
I asked, when he concluded his remarks,
"But are Quarks physical?"
                              You'd think that he
Were someone nearly martyred and I'd said
Our duty's to die peacefully in bed.
He took his glasses off and blinked at me.

Were I John Milton, I would now destroy
This moment of high drama and deploy
A thirty-line Homeric simile.
But I'm not Milton, nor was meant to be.
He put his glasses on, and said, "Of course."

Now, I may be the south end of a horse,
But logically and analogically,
And physically, and metaphysically,
And, if it gets to that, religiously,
And absolutely scientifically,
I don't believe that Quarks can pass the test
Of Being There, and since they're fundamental,
Why, then, the world's a dream, and dreams are mental,
And since in mental matters East or West
I need you for this dream's interpretation—

Stop looking at your watch, for I've divined,
With these two themes uncomfortably combined,
It's time now for the Recapitulation.

Recapitulation

Frankly, I'm disinclined to reassert
The themes my Exposition indicated.
Stuffed shirts there are, and hordes of overrated
Experts who would slay or badly hurt
With airy wave of hand my insights; no,
I will not play to them, I'll not rehash
My song though they with hard and cold cash
Should bribe me, or should tell me where to go.
My complex principles are explicated
Under "Development." So let them laugh:
I'll not permit this section to be half
So convoluted as anticipated.

Cadenza

Sing, Heav'nly Muse, and give me lyric flight,
Give me special effects, give me defiance
To challenge the Academy of Science
On fundamental points, and get them right;
Give me the strength to can the Latinisms,
To forge analogies between the thing
Nature abhors and my apartment; sing
To vanquish literary criticisms
If possible and literary sharks.
And even if you feel submicroscopic
Elements exceed me as a topic,
Please try to back me up regarding Quarks,
Thereby to advocate my metaphor
(Absence the vehicle, physics the tenor)
So that the Universal Void coincides
With showing—I daresay, with showing off—
The consequences of his going off;
By showing everything, in fact, but slides.

Coda

My heart detests, reviles, denounces, loathes
Your absence with a passion like a furnace.
The shirt of love, said Eliot, will burn us;
And normally I'd add, "Love's other clothes
Burn just as badly"—but, because I've bent
A rule or two, I won't extend this figure;
Good taste prevents this piece from getting bigger;
Please see above for everything I meant.

The radio glimmers,
Cities alight in my room
Among cities of books
Stacked in towers.
Each book is a room. In one,
Flaubert affixes the date on the page, July,
And addresses the neglected Louise,
Advising his beauty by mail:
"Read, do not dream." Three months go by.
In my dictionary of saints,
One carries her torn breasts on a plate,
Another washes his severed head
In a fountain, others carry their cities
Before them on trays,
Like fragmented sets of chess.
Below, Gretel peers from a cage.
Above, Lear leans over his map
And chooses the liar;
I press my eyes,
I don't want to read.
But when I tire
Of making shadow-swans who make haste
In the radio light,
And arranging my hairpins in pentacles
And giant alphabets, I need other
Ways of wasting the night.

Through the doorway
The kitchen floor squares make a chessboard

Whose figures have crumbled
To small heaps of dust.
It is morning for you where you sit
In the City of God,
Where every predicament, every desire
Possesses a saint intervening above it.
Saint Barbara, whose father instantly
Turned to a cinder that tangled
Into her broom,
Holds a stony tower
In the crook of one arm.
She presides over gunpowder
And those who die without rites.
You write in a room,
You write rather than dream,
The cities spring up from your pencil point,
Towers, chess, the captured queen
Over whose empty square you preside.
You press on your eyes
As if your head hurt, and the stars
With five points break apart
Into triangles whose corners are swept,
Bent, smoothed into circles
Rolling like wobbling zeroes away.
When you finally look up,
The day will be dark.
I draw crosses, chess,
Then affix names of streets to the lines,
A map, city squares.

When you touched my breasts I saw
Hand shadows, like bird inventions
By Arcimboldo the Marvelous,
Spring to the wall.
A room appeared when I kissed your face
Where with Yaasriel's seventy holy pencils
It is my duty everlastingly
To write your name, without looking up.
But the pencils roll and fall
From my desk in this rented place.
Louise touches the dreaming head
Of her daughter, but reads
The story aloud to the end
Where the bear comes back
And a lost girl has slept in his bed.
Upstairs my neighbors trace
Crossed lines above my head
In vanishing miles,
And I can't fix my eyes on the page
Where Flaubert writes that prose
Is a permanent rage,
Writes to Louise that he'll form
His book as a globe which will hang
"Suspended without visible support"
By the laws of style.
Rain hangs before my eyes
On the weather report.
Like continents beyond the windowsill

Clouds softly tear apart
As if a map were ripped to show
The world is hung on nothing,
He is right. Clouds sail past
The bent head of Louise as she writes back,
A message lost long since.
Countries break apart above the streets.
The window glitters black.
I touch my forehead to the glass.

Read, do not dream.
But my books are towers,
Rooms, dreams where the scenes tangle,
Visible through the stones.
A feather floats up from the page
Where the kitchen maid cries
As she plucks the weeping goose,
Or beats with a broom
White sheets into swans.
On the children-of-royalty's lawns
The beaten hoops stagger
Away from the merciless sticks.
And Lear sits in jail, cut to the brains.
He spreads his drenched map
And waits till it dries,
Then folds it into a pointed hat,
And the faded countries wave in his hair
Like tattered butterflies.

I cannot read,
But I sit at the base of the wall,
Wearing my hands for a hat.

Saint Clare possessed
Bilocal vision, which meant she could see
Events in places where she was not,
The way readers do.
It is morning for you.
You crouch behind your pencil.
If a rhythm branches through the forehead
Like the tree of which the empty page is made,
Gepetto appears with an ax.
He makes a child in which
The tree is hidden.
But Pinocchio's nose reverts
To a tree with leaves where the bird's egg
Rolls like a hoop from the nest and cracks
Into jagged triangles,
And little jaws open soundlessly.
I touch my head as if it were gashed,
Stories reel over the wires,
Narratives when I desire
All things to stare blankly back.

In the hollow squares I write,
"I envy the unfaithful."
They know what to do with the night.
Then I draw the pentacle,

The star they call the endless knot
Because in drawing it the pencil point
Is never lifted once.
The star with five points,
The five paper hats,
A starry crown of triangles
For the betrayed.
And I stare at what I have done,
Beholding in fright
What I have made,

A pyramid wreath, a city of tombs,
And Flaubert writes, "Books grow huge
Like pyramids, and in the end
They almost frighten you."
Louise crumples this into a ball,
And I put my pencil down.
The dust on the kitchen floor:
Crumbled towers, the dust of a vanished crown
In the empty square of the queen.
Upstairs my neighbors pace
And the rain flies down.
Saints look down from the towers
That rise from the paper you spread
Like a map where you write
And do not look up.
I lay the broom in my lap
Like the grizzled head of a saint
With a string for a crown.

Louise pins flowers on her hat
And bursts in on Flaubert.
From the dusty straws,
Like a feather a dead moth floats up
Which I pluck from the air
To set down on the page
Where the words came on
And the lines crossed, streets, city squares
Near the crumpled paper and tower of dreams.
The moth's tiny wrecked skull, its rumpled face
Preside weightless, hushed
Over paper cities:
Little one, in whose papery jaws,
As it is written on paper,
The world is crushed.

SNOW MELTING

Snow melting when I left you, and I took
This fragile bone we'd found in melting snow
Before I left, exposed beside a brook
Where raccoons washed their hands. And this, I know,

Is that raccoon we'd watched for every day.
Though at the time her wild human hand
Had gestured inexplicably, I say
Her meaning now is more than I can stand.

We've reasons, we have reasons, so we say,
For giving love, and for withholding it.
I who would love must marvel at the way
I know aloneness when I'm holding it,

Know near and far as words for live and die,
Know distance, as I'm trying to draw near,
Growing immense, and know, but don't know why,
Things seen up close enlarge, then disappear.

Tonight this small room seems too huge to cross.
And my life is that looming kind of place.
Here, left with this alone, and at a loss
I hold an alien and vacant face

Which shrinks away, and yet is magnified—
More so than I seem able to explain.
Tonight the giant galaxies outside
Are tiny, tiny on my windowpane.

IV

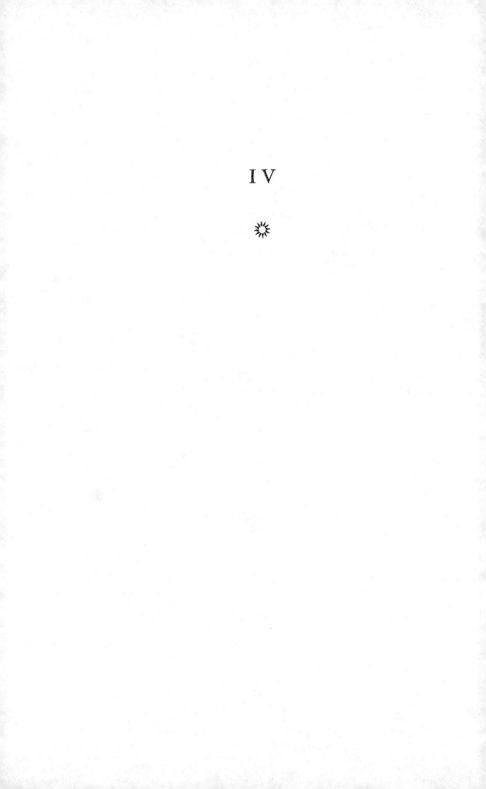

THE HEAVENLY FEAST

Simone Weil, 1909–1943

Only the stones at first
Seem to have a part in this,
And the little height of the grass
As it gains a fraction-inch

By gripping the shallow soil
With all the shocking might
Of hunger and of thirst,
As if the soil itself

Were all that's left on earth.
I think the grass alone
Can hold within its grasp
What matters to it most,

And still it looks bereft,
And famished as the stones.
I watch a stream of moths
Proceeding on their ways,

They carve out tortuous paths
As if they were intent
On entering unseen
And ever-smaller doors.

So four years into the war,
And cut off from the ones
Whose circumstance you felt
And suffering as yours,

You carved yourself a path
Through ever-narrowing doors
Of hunger and of thirst,
And entered them day by day,

Refusing all at first
But that ration of food
Your people could obtain
Behind the lines in France,

And then refusing that,
From summer into fall
You cut your ration back
To send your part to them,

Your part diminishing
To rations cut in half
And cut in half again,
And then nothing at all

But water at the last
Sipped for the nurse's sake,
You finally lacked the strength
Even to lift your hands:

Father, I cannot stand
To think of them and eat.
Send it to them, it is theirs.
Send this food for them,

For my people still in France.
And turned your face away,
As famished as the grass.
Only the stones at first

Seem to have a part in this,
And the little height of the grass
As it gains a fraction-inch.
But hidden in the grass

As if the grass itself
Were giving out a cry,
I overhear the finch
Begin her native rhyme

And toil to paraphrase
Her version of your words.
It seems she tries and tries
Until the words come clear,

It is theirs, she seems to say,
Or that is what I hear,
And again: It is theirs, it is theirs.
And the plover joins in praise

With her fluttering, murmured prayers:
Send it to them, it is theirs.
And the blackbirds breaking wide
Take it up in their dialects

To sing you in their way,
I swear I can hear the words,
Send it to them, they say,
Send it to them, it is theirs,

Then all the birds of the air
Give thanks above your grave,
As if they were your cause
And those you meant to save,

As if the birds were there
In attendance at the end,
And, seeing the sacrifice
Had borne your body up,

So wasted as it was,
To your chair in Paradise,
And saw, before they fled,
Your first breathtaking act

Before the heavenly feast,
The bread set at your place:
To refuse to eat till none
On earth has less than you,

Though God in pity take
Your hands and lift them toward
His table for your sake.
Father, they have no food,

Send it to them, it is theirs.
And the birds returning here
Give tongue to what they've heard,
They tell the grass and stones

And the stream of moths who carve
Their tortuous paths in the air.
But how in giving thanks
Can we calculate the worth

Of one who chose to starve?
You held within your grasp
Our hunger and our thirst.
And the little height of the grass

As it gains a fraction-inch
Seems to have a part in this.
It grips with a shocking might
What matters to the last,

As if the soil itself
Were all that's left on earth,
And all the earth were held
Within its famished grasp.

ADVENT CALENDAR

Bethlehem in Germany,
Glitter on the sloping roofs,
Breadcrumbs on the windowsills,
Candles in the Christmas trees,
Hearths with pairs of empty shoes:
Panels of Nativity
Open paper scenes where doors
Open into other scenes,
Some recounted, some foretold.
Blizzard-sprinkled flakes of gold
Gleam from small interiors,
Picture-boxes in the stars
Open up like cupboard doors
In a cabinet Jesus built.

Southern German villagers,
Peasants in the mica frost,
See the comet streaming down,
Heavenly faces, each alone,
Faces lifted, startled, lost,
As if lightning lit the town.

Sitting in an upstairs window
Patiently the village scholar
Raises his nearsighted face,
Interrupted by the star.
Left and right his hands lie stricken
Useless on his heavy book.
When I lift the paper door

In the ceiling of his study
One canary-angel glimmers,
Flitting in the candelabra,
Peers and quizzes him: Rabbi,
What are the spheres surmounted by?
But his lips are motionless.
Child, what are you asking for?
Look, he gazes past the roofs,
Gazes where the bitter North,
Stretched across the empty place,
Opens door by door by door.

This is childhood's shrunken door.
When I touch the glittering crumbs,
When I cry to be admitted,
No one answers, no one comes.

And the tailor's needle flashes
In midair with thread pulled tight,
Stitching a baptismal gown.
But the gown, the seventh door,
Turns up an interior
Hidden from the tailor's eyes:
Baby presents like the boxes
Angels hold on streets and stairways,
Wooden soldier, wooden sword,
Chocolate coins in crinkled gold,
Hints of something bought and sold,
Hints of murder in the stars.
Baby's gown is sown with glitter
Spread across the tailor's lap.
Up above his painted ceiling

Baby mouse's skeleton
Crumbles in the mouse's trap.

Leaning from the cliff of heaven,
Indicating whom he weeps for,
Joseph lifts his lamp above
The infant like a candle-crown.
Let my fingers touch the silence
Where the infant's father cries.
Give me entrance to the village
From my childhood where the doorways
Open pictures in the skies.
But when all the doors are open,
No one sees that I've returned.
When I cry to be admitted,
No one answers, no one comes.
Clinging to my fingers only
Pain, like glitter bits adhering,
When I touch the shining crumbs.

SUPERNATURAL LOVE

My father at the dictionary-stand
Touches the page to fully understand
The lamplit answer, tilting in his hand

His slowly scanning magnifying lens,
A blurry, glistening circle he suspends
Above the word "Carnation." Then he bends

So near his eyes are magnified and blurred,
One finger on the miniature word,
As if he touched a single key and heard

A distant, plucked, infinitesimal string,
"The obligation due to every thing
That's smaller than the universe." I bring

My sewing needle close enough that I
Can watch my father through the needle's eye,
As through a lens ground for a butterfly

Who peers down flower-hallways toward a room
Shadowed and fathomed as this study's gloom
Where, as a scholar bends above a tomb

To read what's buried there, he bends to pore
Over the Latin blossom. I am four,
I spill my pins and needles on the floor

Trying to stitch "Beloved" X by X.
My dangerous, bright needle's point connects
Myself illiterate to this perfect text

I cannot read. My father puzzles why
It is my habit to identify
Carnations as "Christ's flowers," knowing I

Can give no explanation but "Because."
Word-roots blossom in speechless messages
The way the thread behind my sampler does

Where following each X I awkward move
My needle through the word whose root is love.
He reads, "A pink variety of Clove,

Carnatio, the Latin, meaning flesh."
As if the bud's essential oils brush
Christ's fragrance through the room, the iron-fresh

Odor carnations have floats up to me,
A drifted, secret, bitter ecstasy,
The stems squeak in my scissors, *Child, it's me,*

He turns the page to "Clove" and reads aloud:
"The clove, a spice, dried from a flower-bud."
Then twice, as if he hasn't understood,

He reads, "From French, for *clou*, meaning a nail."
He gazes, motionless. "Meaning a nail."
The incarnation blossoms, flesh and nail,

I twist my threads like stems into a knot
And smooth "Beloved," but my needle caught
Within the threads, *Thy blood so dearly bought*,

The needle strikes my finger to the bone.
I lift my hand, it is myself I've sewn,
The flesh laid bare, the threads of blood my own,

I lift my hand in startled agony
And call upon his name, "Daddy Daddy"—
My father's hand touches the injury

As lightly as he touched the page before,
Where incarnation bloomed from roots that bore
The flowers I called Christ's when I was four.

A

GILDED LAPSE

OF TIME

(1992)

☀

FOR MY HUSBAND,
ROBERT

PART ONE

A GILDED LAPSE OF TIME

(*Ravenna*)

1. The Mausoleum of Galla Placidia

When love was driven back upon itself,
When a lapse, where my life should have been,
Opened like a breach in the wall, and I stood
At a standstill before the gate built with mud,
I thought my name was spoken and I couldn't reply—
Even knowing that when you hear your name
It's a soul on the other side who is grieving
For you, though you're never told why.

Among the hallowed statues of dead stalks
I stood, where the rosebush was abandoned by
The pruning shears, among the stumps of brambles
Near the muddy door to the next life.
There was a rubbish mound at the ancient gate
And a broken branch the gardeners had tossed
Toward the leaf pile, scattering its gold dust
Before the doorway carved, as if into a hillside,
Into a frozen room raised in the desolate
Outskirts of Byzantium, where now an industrial zone
Pressed toward the porch of an ancient church
Built in the fulfillment of a vow,
Where the Byzantines would lay aside
Their musical instruments in order to enter
The sanctuary unaccompanied; I stood

Uncertain at the threshold of a pile
Of enigmatic, rose-colored brick, a tomb
A barbarian empress built for herself
That conceals within its inauspicious,
Shattered-looking vault the whirl of gold,
The inflooding realm we may only touch
For one instant with a total leap of the heart—
Like the work of the bees who laid aside
Their holy, inner craft because the Lord
Whistled for them, and they fled
To Him, but long ago, leaving behind
These unfinished combs from biblical antiquity
We are forbidden to touch, still deep
In the wood's heart, still dripping on the ground.

2

Then a tour guide beckoned me in,
And lifted her flashlight beam to the low vault
Of the Second Rome, brushing the white,
Fifth-century, barbarian stars with gilt,
And I could hear the snowflakes gathering overhead
In the treasure vaults of snow from another age,
In vaults where the snowflake is begotten,
Where angels crowded toward us, inquisitive,
In Paradise, where they'd long ago forgotten
That God repented after He made man,

Where the doves had built their summer palaces
With green grass plucked from underneath
The bare feet of the blessed, and gold glass glowed
As if embers from the imperial furnaces
Had breathed behind the walls, were breathing
From the sphere where love is kindled,
Even if that sphere was broken long before
Our births—but when I pressed
My palm against the uneven, glittering stones,
To the touch they were winter-desolate.

Then objects in heaven began to throb.
Though overlaid with your planets, Dante,
Your stack of nine heavens, your God the Father
Above the hollow spheres, and the eight hundred stars
Drawn into the plaster by the Pictor Imaginarius
That still throb in a Byzantine horoscope
No one will ever bother to cast again—

Still, the hammered gold in rooms all through
Byzantium conceals the pictureless underworlds
Of mortar slathered by the workmen's trowels,
And the vaults' dead spaces are held up
By supporting empty earthenware jars
Still intact, still holding up the stars
In the dome-shaped fog of gold that stands
As motionless as the huge globe you walked
From end to end, beginning here below—
Not like those vessels God had wanted to use
In creating the world but which broke in His hands.

3

Dante, in Paradise, as you climbed,
Earth was only a word, earth was only the place
Where you had died, where you had hidden
The *Paradiso*'s ending behind a wall
And it began to molder after you died.
You'd long ago left behind the cliffs of hell,
The immaterial mountain, the sphere of the moon,
But the sight of His face, of the book of love unbound
And scattering its leaves, you hid away
In a blank, unmarked place on the wall beside
Your deathbed, where your descendants could scrape
With a knife or a broken branch, not daring
To say aloud what they were looking for—
The ending, pointed out in a dream.

4

I have visited every fountain in the guidebook,
And loitered at the crumbling rims
Of baptistry fonts whose quarter-inch
Of water lies gilded beneath
The ceiling mosaic's tremorous, rhythmic hymns,
Where God is a word written into the ceiling
Under planets shining even by day—

And outdoors in the city traffic,
I've crossed and recrossed these city squares
As if I were pacing them off, as if
I had dropped everything to come and look,
As if there were nothing to do but thumb
The index for the names of goddesses
Who cried at these sites and springs arose
Beneath their feet, so that, ever since,
Throughout the mosaics across Ravenna's ceilings
A streak of blue perpetually flows,
An upwelling crux of radiance in the grasses
That draws animals in search of healing,

Stags whose horns flash as they bend to drink,
Peacocks taking refuge at the springs,
Lambs with drops of water on their muzzles,
Doves mesmerized at the edge of a birdbath
Where a parched leaf whirls at the brilliant cliff
The water makes along its edge before it falls
Among holes like dried-up waterfalls
That wore channels through the bricks, breaking open

Upon ever deeper, ever hastier depictions,
Pictures sealed within pictures, of water boiling
Behind the bricks before it swamped the room
With a glistening mirage, dry to the touch

Though once these streets were canals, once inhabitants
Complained in the civic registers of terrible
Smells stirred up by the bargemen's poles,
Once the waters rose so high the citizens
Were drowned in their houses, in floods whose chronicles
Lay open in my room last night, depicted
On parched paper as a succession of tides
Boiling through the dark ages—a deluge
Marked by a flood tablet on a street corner,

Where the fountains have lain choked for centuries
As if Justinian, with a reckless word,
Had expelled the water from the city, so that
The fountains also of the deep and the windows
Of heaven were stopped, and the rain from heaven
Was restrained—and he heard in his far-off rooms
On the other side of Asia Minor
Ravenna's blackbirds crying and crying for rain,
Beating at the eaves for a drop of water,
His palace ceilings haunted by their cries for mercy,
And in remorse had ordered his engineers
To inscribe a dome the size of Calvary
With Latin letters spelled in gold rain,
Hinting at other, unmarked deluges reeling

Past the rooflines in churches across the city
Where angels lift the drapes aside to show
Yet another fountain pictured in the ceiling.

5. San Vitale

Now in a gilded apse the celestial globe
Has rolled to the end of an invisible rope
And come to rest on a cliff in a blue-green garden.
I look up, as if nothing had killed my hope,
At a blue sphere, buoyant in the sixth-century tides
Still surging and dying away through San Vitale,
Where a spring has glinted in the numinous
Fresh-cut grass for more than a millennium
And never has evaporated or flooded over,
Though it is cracked in a million places, a dried
Streambed the Messiah has walked in search of water.
He leans back, white-faced, to say *I thirst*
Among rosebushes He threw His robe across
In exhaustion and thereby carelessly blessed—

Bright traces of those ancient floods
Shine above the vanished altar, fed by the old motif
Of four rivers whose names I am unsure of,
Four heavenly rivers pouring overhead
From the next world, backward into this,
But they shiver and draw back, suspended above our heads,
Hanging, in the mosaics, like icicles
Unable to pour their healing waters over us,

Though glinting through a hole at my feet
There is a flood remnant, reflected in the apse,
As if the Samaritan woman's water jar
Had been hurled against the wall, and still was dripping
Into the long-lost relics' burial place;

[145]

Or it may be only a freshly washed floor
Whose little lakes are dashed from a metal pail
And swept around by the custodian's mop—
I cannot tell. But they say the ice-cold well
Of martyrdom brims into the present here,
They say this is the hollow-hidden font
Where fragments of lost names illegibly
Shiver behind an ancient grille.

6

There the human being is the vision all my life
I was tutored in, there the *imago Dei* wavers
Above the flooded, inaccessible crypt,
A radiant blur, reflected, elusive among
Supporting columns knee-deep in cold water
Routinely drained by an invisible pump—
We are water that is spilled on the ground
Where Jesus ripples outward, His hand outstretched;
His palm lies open, lifted and upheld
On the jet of an invisible fountain
Cohering from an undulating hush,
Though hints of other, higher, atrocious waters
Tower in the apse's gilt peripheries,
Where a thousand years may intervene between
One glimpse and another, between the coming to
Of the water-resurrected image and what
My heart still struggles with, and still cannot
Surrender up to you,

Messiah, banished to an apse so crushed beneath
A Visigoth's pillaging axe, you felt the blow,
So crushed even the Empress could take fright—
She whose deeds panicked the chronicler—
Even she could dash the stolen suffering cup
At the fountain, and raise her cupped
Palms to catch the cascading hexameter-streams
Of Byzantine hymns, engulfed by the stone sea,
Praying with hidden face, standing apart:

Messiah, do not withdraw your hand from me.
Messiah, looking back where we have gathered
On the stone floor—looking through crazed gold,
As if you'd raised yourself to gaze at us,
Astonished, through a broken window's heart.

7

Far below I rest my hand against the stones
The workmen laid in 547, when they believed
A hollow sphere encompassed us, when they thought
That there must exist spheres, made
Of the fifth essence, situated in the depth
Of the universe, and moving there,
Some higher up, some arranged below them,
Some larger, some smaller, some hollow,
And some massive within the hollow ones,
To which the planets are fastened,
Each axis fixed on the surface of the one
Surrounding it, and seven planets wheeling
Under God's omnipresent shadow, where now

At the scaffolding before the Sacrifice of Isaac
The aproned workers of a restoration team
Lean from their wooden balcony, urging me
To climb a ladder through the scaffolding
To join those angels seated in the cold church
At a feast table beneath a leafy oak,
Three angels who turn their eyes away
Lest they come face to face with God breaking a law
In the white gaps the sacred text still haunts,
Lest they witness Abraham's unrecorded response,
Lest they see his knife raised for the death stroke—
I hear the world brake on its axis
And come to a halt at the foot of the wall
I rest my hand on; I hear a rope wobble, lashing
The globe back and forth in a scourge of gold snow

That parts on the sight of other ceilings,
Other chains, other heights from which
Other worlds hang, and a book creaks open
In the stars above Isaac's head:
Oh, slam this book shut! God, do not show us!
But the angels do not look, scrupulous in
Honoring the law in Paradise that no one may
Observe the suffering of humans here below—
Not even in that ancient time when God
Reached down to interrupt the sacrifice,
As if He hadn't meant to hurt us so—
We'd not yet driven Him into the high gilt corner
Of a tesserae-shattered wall where a workman
Touches a flake of gold leaf in the hem
Of His threadbare gown with a tweezers woefully small.

I sit on the scaffolding near where God
Is deafened, haggard on His mercy seat,
The stars around Him covered with black cloths
Lest they hold His dying day in awe,
The lower section of His throne hidden partially
With scaffolding and drapes, as if He had wrapped up
The black, jagged star that overhung Byzantium,
Wound it up in a cloth and stowed it beneath His throne.
Then *look no more upon't!* Then *pluck it off!*
Our fault has aged you, driven you off, our fault
Has pressed you into this inaccessible vault
Where you are the Lord of a stone floor
That boiled up so long ago you can't recall,
Where you've forgotten that you made the world
To boil at its heart with boiling stone—

Overhead, the scribe Isaiah holds a scroll,
And though the mortifying coal, the supernatural ember,
Had scorched his lips—
Isaiah gazes down from a gold-leafed tower
At those of us stranded in the aftermath,
He gazes down from the heights of his poetry,
He gazes down as if his poetry had not driven
Jesus along the muddy path.

Lord, we cannot discern
The guilt of our callings—
Let me turn away, at fault, and overawed;
Let me say, *You are still my Lord and my God*,
Let me say I am unable to ascertain
The guilt of poetry, and leave a prayer scribbled
In the gold room where the written word
Presses us back—
You are the God
Of a word we have not learned,
And the *verbum visibilum* really does
Flicker in the gilt fog of the apse
Where it once burned.

Now in alabaster-mullioned galleries
The mosaics are a bank of gold snow
Deposited by a half a million afternoons,
A twinkling reef of crud,
A cliff of lowering cold that pushes
Toward the ladder's edge, where
One world passes into the next as the earth
Slowly revolves away from the sinking apse
Beyond the scaffold ledge,
Where God's hand hangs empty above
The depiction of frightful laws
As if He tried to plunge
His hand into a bank of gold snow
Covered with grime,
To grasp at least a handful

Of Creation, to remember it by,
But what He touches thaws,
And starts to trickle through itself,
Then streams off through His hand,
Downward, through the gilded lapse of time.

In the cypress zone behind your tomb,
Between two worlds, there was a gash
Where *the creation was subjected*
To futility, like a hole
Where a cross was planted once,
Like a dead fountain, dismantled
And carted off in the spoil wagons
Of Charlemagne,
Like a lost foundation dug up by a dog,
Like a hole dug out by rain.

Now, in the grass, what's left
Is the buried pavement
Long since broken up,
Numbered, and hauled off
To a museum crypt,
And the foundations of the bell tower,

From the time when
The grime-scrubbed
Throne of Maximian
Was merely an empty ivory chair,
Merely a throne abandoned in a grassy field
With a great crack running across the back,
A gash inflicted
In a crisis so severe
In the wake of the invasions they'd lost track
Of calendars, planetary
Epicycles, holy years,

Though marauders spared
The purple cushion without price,
Fashioned in Ravenna's silk shops,
That loomed on the otherwise empty throne
Of the Redeemer—
Now the narrow puddles
In the thorn brake are radiant shrouds
Left lying in the grass overnight,
Shining in the garden
As if Ravenna's
Citizens were resurrected here.

With drenched stockings,
Ankle-deep in wet grass,
I lower my foot to fathom
A depression in the grass,
Like a biblical cleft
In the rock, in an oceanside town
From which even the ocean has withdrawn
Beyond a marsh
Whose fever plague swept
You off, though now the sea is four miles away—
Where the Greek Exarchs built
Their guardhouses and privies, their furnaces
For glassworks, their sewer drains
And smokestacks, their chapels evanesced

In a whirl of rain
That hurls itself from that age to my feet,

Among the empty sarcophagi
Strewn around
The medieval grounds, where the Judgment
Tore off the humblest stone lids
But left undisturbed the rich men's
Marble graves, where the resurrection
Is only for marble caterpillars
Sculpted in their shrouds,

Though nearly induced,
Nearly transmogrified,
Nearly pulsing like butterflies
Shaken from a sack
Into the freezing church,
Like rhymes you shook into blizzards
Still circling back
Six hundred years above Ravenna
And never alighting
Among the glittering floors and marble lakes
Of monuments that sheltered you.
Rain slants, crashing into puddles
Where, among the lost graves of the poor,
I lean over, looking into
The mirrored, northern edge

Of the Western Roman Empire grown over
With stiff grass,
Where the long-vanished basilicas
From here to Classe

Still waver like images
Rendered in shrouds,
Petriana, San Severo, and the one so long-lost
Its name is absent even from
The ancient documents,

Vanished apses,
Buoyant above the water table,
Where the bloody story still
Is recounted overhead
In blurry detail,
Where the executioner stands
Like a rose sprung up at the foot of the cross
Wearing a mask of bees
In the circle of those
Who stood together on the Mount of Paradise,
And Jesus wears on His head
The excruciating radiance.

But when I bend down
To peer through the overgrown grass,
Speeding toward me suddenly rivers of butterflies
Undulate into my eyes
So that I quickly straighten up—
There is only a road laid through a gray cloud
To a marsh, a difficult approach
To a sagging mound of bricks, and a few bushes
I can't name, scraggling in a dripping lane,
And grass running toward the docks

Of the imperial fleet,
Silted over, or floated off across the Adriatic;

I lower my foot
As if a holy stream were running past,
As if the puddle held a rain-bright cross,
Then reach down to touch
This fragment of the northern hemisphere,
To riffle and disturb
An empty place the rain is rending,
A hole spreading above the world,
A drift of dark reflected—

Not the river like a strip of light
Into which you plunged your face, in Paradise,
Letting it cascade from your lashes,
Only a raindrop
On my lashes into which
I look in time to see
A black star drawing near
Plunge past my peripheral sight,
And disappear.

In English *world* is an isolated sound,
With an unmistakable, audible, inward whirl,
Tilted on a hum that rhymes with itself,
Revolving when we speak it, then ceasing to spin.
We may founder before it, stranded before the page
Where we gaze at it from above,
Though if we say *worldworldworldworldworld*
We can feel it beginning to spin around
Its axis, then brake to a halt
When we turn our attention away. You believed
We intuit the sound of the spheres, Dante,
When God touches our ears. *Ephphatha. Be thou opened.*

For you the earth was motionless, silent,
Suspended, except that it gaped with hell,
With a distant reverberation underfoot,
A din you heard rising from the world's
Shattered insides where those without hope
Rave and beat on the ground.

But stranded on the cliff's edge
Of your death mask, and older than you were
That morning when you began to take the way down
Into hidden, gigantic dimensions,
Over the sides of diminishing terraces
I can't bring myself to peer from—
Here on earth, in the room above
The temple they built on your tomb,
I circle around

And reappear, an apparition in midair
In the glass case where your death mask shows
The likeness of a man who, closing his eyes,
Holds still in order to discern
A very faint sound.

Lying among gifts from continents you didn't see
Even from heaven, and a sack of laurel leaves
D'Annunzio hefted here in homage
To the original withered remnants of a crown
They found among your bones, like a lost branch

Fallen from that ancient gunnysack of thorns
Cain trundles on his back across the moon,
But someone else's moon, not ours, one of
Those moons which circles . . . Jupiter . . . Neptune . . .

Your mask lies, petrified into a bronze model
Of lunar cliffs at whose base you were stranded
And could ascend only by having a dream of ascent;

This mask, a speechless record of the moment that,
When shining forcefully upon you God
Beat back the weakness of your gaze, you
Were blinded by the radiance of love, and you left behind

This mask—as if you'd groped your way back here
Across a barrier of thorns, to find
A makeshift throne of rock, and took your seat
In a city of empty thrones and headless crowns,

Still wearing the lopsided, shattered wreath
Ravenna crowned you with after your death,
When you were lifted through Ravenna's streets—
The laurel crown refused, withheld, forgone,

Now scattered on a wooden museum shelf
Before your blinded gaze, you who were crowned—
Before you crossed the threshold, where you saw
The stars grow larger, brighter than they ever looked
From Florence or Ravenna—lord of yourself.

But these remnants from the tree of poetry
Could be the leaves you gathered up
After that accident in the second wood,
After that wound, inflicted inadvertently,
That welling in the bowl of an injury
You could not stanch or bind with a rag,
That babbling injury at the root of speech
From a speechless depth you'd torn into that soul:
Why do you break me? Why do you tear me?
Something whose suffering you understood
But thought too sacred to be said aloud.
And as for me, once I had seen that seeping
At the root of that outcry, I kept to myself,
Afraid that if I spoke, my tongue would
Touch those mutilated words, I was afraid
That if I spoke I would taste blood: Don't tear
The leaves off the tree of nonexistence,
Don't pull them bleeding and crying from the branch!
Leave the unconceived alone, unborn!
Leave them hidden above this smear of blood!
If you would love them, do this much for them,
To let them be. Or that is what I heard
When I thought poetry was love, and I had
Sickened of poetry.

I would lay open before my God
That nine and twentieth year of mine age.
I would lay open those years that I could not
Speak. Years I could only thumb the page
Into featureless velvet, unraveling the bleary gilt
Where the kingdom had glinted but guttered out,
Where I copied out your verses by hand
In a foreign language, and as I wrote I could see
Those rhymes throb down the length of the page
And that sound—a glimpse of that sound,
After which everything I had scribbled
In my own hand came to a weightless bundle,
But what foundered beyond the page was more
Than I could lift, more than could be enshadowed
Even in a private script in the margins—

Though here on earth letters
Do not cast shadows, as you did,
Dumbfounding the dead,
Still, lying across
That white realm of silence,
Such pictures are formed
I would lower a ruler into hell
To measure its depth,

But when I run my palm over the page
Those hovering magnitudes evaporate,
Leaving flat paper, without depth;
My fingertips can feel nothing there,
Or else the letters
Have joined their shadows,
And cleave to them,
Spelling out in the white silence
A black, intangible script,
A catechism of existence without objects,
Though I read to myself, moving my lips—

As if I could take my mind off
That outpouring from the branches,
Where you tore the letters
From silence, as if to hurt that soul,
As if purposely to draw
A scent of bloodspill,
Where my pencil
Unwittingly had inscribed a black star

In the margin, beside the verse that pours
Its weeping question out to you—then
I turned away from that sudden cry
In the black-leaved void,
Leaving you there, speechless in the wood;
I turned away
To scramble out of those deepening
Cliffs that hang at our feet;
I grasped at a branch,
And wounded it, tearing it
To pull myself up—

Though if I could have clenched
That crud of leaves in my fist,
Until a sludge of gold seeped to the surface,
I would have pressed the leaves
In reverence to my lips.

Then the evening bell struck thirteen in your honor
And I returned to the sound of my own lips.
But when the museum guard hauled shut at my heel
The heavy, consecutive doors they've set
Into your tomb, hauling with all his weight
As if he were the seraph responsible
For the operation of the great wheels, for
The turning of the slowest of the spheres—
I heard a deeper set of doors slam shut,

A sound reverberating outside the walls of poetry,
As if the doors of the kingdom had closed behind me
With that sound you could not transcribe
After you'd crossed the threshold of the dead
And entered a gate from which you promised
Never to look back, no matter what,

As the doors slammed shut,
And you let your thoughts revolve
Around the bliss of leaving your life behind,
Of clinging in your ascent, and looking up,
Forgetting earth with every step you took—

1 8

Dante, in Paradise, as you climbed,
From the starry paths you must have seen
The mansions that stood uninhabited

In empty Florence, grass pushing through the floors,
The stairway to your father's house become
A stairway up to other people's doors

In city squares with unfamiliar names;
You must have seen the city's marble squares
Crowded with strangers and their descendants,

Roads choked with future people streaming away,
Their backs to you, and if they turned around,
You would not know them; you must have seen

Their lives were simply other people's wars—
And, farther back, you must have seen yourself
Driven back upon a sequence of nativities

In stony hill towns, an enemy of Florence,
Traveling west to east, through Golgothas
In blizzards of gold, on peeling walls,

In shadowy plaster, in smoky oils
Shadowing forth, the letter X formed
Out of angels revolving above all those

Upturned faces in driving rain joined by your own.
But in fact you often loitered there alone,
Peering up, not into the heavens as you thought,

But into the low, smoke-blackened ceilings;
In fact, you often paced, not the terraces
Of Purgatory, but only your borrowed study,

Looking down, not from Paradise, but from
The second story, into a dreary province
Lit from the north and stretching through a marsh

Among Roman sarcophagi, in a backwater
Formerly a capital, barren of ideas;
You stood stock-still, not in the shadowless

Grass with angels, but in the icy garden lanes
Of the Count who sheltered you, still postulating
The existence of another heaven outside

The heaven of the stars, still intuiting
The glint of the primum mobile flashing east
To west with that beautiful shimmering, that trepidation,

Whose movement is swift beyond all comprehension,
Without which the planet Saturn would be hidden
From every place on earth for fifteen years,

The planet Jupiter for six, the planet Mars
For nearly a year . . . *She had lived in this world*
For the length of time in which the heaven of

The fixed stars had circled one twelfth of a degree
Towards the East . . .
But even then your poem began to unwind

Its road before your feet, along which you hurried
Through the marsh-plain back to Florence,
The road where you anxiously hailed and overtook

Events, conversations, persons long dead,
Other exiles of other people's cities,
As at your back, along the Adriatic coast,

The sunset's whirling towers would collapse
And buckle through the gates they tore
Into themselves, melting sideways into the sea,

Floating there in swirls of scarlet-lilac,
Then darken and go under silently,
And then: *the luminous sphere of Mars,*

As if a city-state would turn its powers
Of banishment against itself so easily,
And melt away, so you could see the stars.

But as for me, standing
Among blank rocks,
After that door was shut, I turned
And hurried away. After that sound,
I hurried along the road
Toward my hotel, beneath the heavenly city
Visible when one emerges into the night,
Past the Law Giver's
Holy domes, where He promulgates
The laws of bliss whereby we are meant
To turn our backs on the pain
Of the condemned when we're forgiven;

I hurried past
The utopian arcades of the entrance
To the Basilica Metropolitana,
The disbanded workshops
For the manufacture of gold glass,
Past numberless empty tombs
And acres of church floors
Still strewn with gold-glass cubes
Like splinters of the spheres
Lying crushed beneath our feet,
Past street signs pointing
To Theodoric's dome,
A cracked sphere
Fallen from the sixth century
Into a ring of desolate suburbs,
Perpetually shrouded in its Ostrogothic dusk;

I hurried beneath the stars
To my hotel,
To the reading lamp's
Blindness-inducing aureole,
The intangible, brilliant sphere
Through which I could pass my hand,
Watching it float above
Your Purgatory, your dream weightless as
You walk the world from end to end,
Then touch the starry paths.

But when I turned out the lamp,
And stood a moment on the cold tiles in my room
As if underneath that roof from the dark ages,
Where I had tried to shake off
The old chill, though night,
In a rented room, is a kingdom too—
Then I turned to my God;
I looked outside;
Beyond the window ledge of my room,
Above the roofs of the city,
The curving height

Where the night creation glittered—
I looked, to try to fix it in my sight,
I raised my eyes to the high wheels,
I tried to turn with you to see
That point at which the fixed stars
Twinkle in translations,

Where one motion and another cross,
Where east and west mingle
With unfamiliar orbits and constellations
Before which we could grow
Forgetful, as if our lives and deeds
No longer mattered—were it not that
We still hear that weeping there below.

Then Gabriel sent down a dream that I stood
Holding a broken-off branch in the wood's heart,
And turning around, I saw the gate built with mud

From the other side, and flights of stairs above my head—
I had passed through it, and the branch I found myself
Holding shrank in my arms and withered away.

Fastened above the gate, a broken honeycomb
Like the concave interior of a death mask
Knocked from an ancestral frieze

Gaped: I had struck it—I had meant only
To open your book, to study poetry's empty beauty,
Not to rest my hand on two featureless tablets of wax

Fashioned with honeycombs in the age of kings,
The combs a poet touches to his lips,
Seeking to cross the threshold, to signify

A sacred conversation. I had broken
The reliquary of the bee, where she had sifted
Her yellow powder through melismatic generations,

Worlds, numberless lifetimes, seeking to finish
Her combs, to mix a flower-dust paste and fix
One drop to the blank mask of her catacomb,

To the brink of a miniature chasm—we are meant
To open a hive with reverence, but instead
I had broken the hive apart with a branch, and worse,

I had left the honeycomb dripping on the ground
In the wood's heart, a profanity
Of waste, and the bees whirled into my ears

Their endless sequences, their burning rhymes
I groped among for what I meant to say.
Angels were there, and one of them turned

And struck me when I spoke, and I lifted my hand
And touched blood on my mouth, and then I saw
They were holding an impression from your face—

Or rather a heavy honeycomb, and your words
Were a stream of bees floating toward me in sunlight.
When I opened your book I thought you spoke,

Or else it was Gabriel lifting to my lips
A tablespoon of golden, boiling smoke
So wounding to my mouth I turned my back

On the source of poetry, and then I woke.

PART TWO

CRUX

OF

RADIANCE

ANNUNCIATION

Rumors lash the angel's robes
Into transitory statues
Madly overturned,
But they disappear without breaking.

The grasshopper standing near the wall
Like a remnant of the plague
Has turned her face away,
Quadrupled in shadow on the bricks,
Undisturbed by what takes place in heaven,
She fiddles her psalm of grief
Again and again, seventy times seven,
Letting her composition unfurl
Waves of black oxygen.

And the paper wasp has left off
Weaving a death mask
For Augustus, in a secret place,
And arrived to touch the wall uneasily,
Seeking a way to blindly touch
The angel's face,
To prepare for a future measuring.

Outside, in a narrow court of stone,
Where a broom leans against a heap
Of debris, where Rome is piled up on Rome,
King Herod is a beggar in the lane,
And the handful of gravel he
Offers with an averted face,
In his outstretched palm,
Was once Jerusalem—

The gravel of ritual objects,
Temple remnants, broken tablets, a handful
Of pulsing coals whose catacombs
Are airy mazes where human cries
Were torn out by the roots,
Torn word by word,
Like gold nuggets from the Roman mines,
But silent now, twinkling,
As if nothing had occurred.

3

Herod, trying to build
A crooked door
Out of King David's wrecked harp
Looted from the Temple,
Sets the harp frame upright,
Then turns to gesture others in,
But discovers himself alone
In the little Jewish village.
And the harp is an opening
Through which angels have swarmed
And disappeared from the roads;
The harp is an opening like the mouth
Of King David, upon which a speechless
Psalm is formed.

4

Where is everyone?
They lie captured
In the holds of ships,
They are stuffed in a narrow hole,
They are slaves in an alien marketplace,
And horses drag them by the hair.
They are sold off to the mines.
The last person is slain
In the bath and there is
No one left to put to the test.

There was a battle
No one bothered to record
Since there were troubles enough.
An upheaval on such a scale that
Afterwards, through the temple porches
Strange planets from a glittery hoard
Were swimming past.
There were heavy rains
Through which the people
Struggled north.

Leaning against the wall,
An axe handle Joseph made
For an axe that Azrael seized
From Joseph's hands
And wielded so recently
The vine blossoms still gasp
Along the blade.

When Azrael entered the road,
All the brooms withdrew
From the stoops.
All the doors
Slammed shut in the streets.
One by one the grinders
Ceased to grind the grain.
When Azrael passed by a house,
All the knives were reground,
The pottery broken and quickly swept away—
In Azrael's path,
Shattered plates in a mound.
Now, if a loom's shuttle was found
To be carved out of wood that had grown
From the grove of ground
Over which the angel had passed,
The shuttle would be destroyed.

But Azrael halts, and says to the air:
I too must drink from a broken cup.
I too must sit at the choked fountain.
I too have a fragment of the void
Lodged in my brain.
He fingers broken threads that hang
Like relics of the silenced harps
The worshippers left on the stairs.
I too have pain.

With each word he speaks,
As if words could break
Distant palaces apart,
The shadowy house
Before which Augustus sits
Crumbles onto its stairs.
Then the court becomes
A haunt of birds.
The law, merely a statement. Merely words.
His face merely a cast
The air had taken with a smothering
Handful of plaster at the moment
His illness took hold.

He sits in front of his house
With his hand held out,
Obeying the dictates of a dream,
Grown suddenly old.
Visible in the distance,
Behind his head, smoke issues
From the altars of Mars,
Venus, Saturn.
In the heart of diseased Rome,
Men hold buckets in the air
At the foot of smashed aqueducts.
Foreign deities are lumps of black ice
Beneath straw crowns,

Deities, skirted by nameless roads
Battered with hoofprints, who
Melt in the heavy rains—
The first Rome,
Dimly recalled from a soldier's
Drawing in the dirt,
Now up to its ankles in muddy lanes.

But Gabriel's blood foams in his chest.
He cannot bring himself to look.
This remnant of the bowl of reeling,
Stairways, the legendary well,
Back alleys, low doorways,
Even the starry regions overhead—
All are gravel, destined
To be recounted only in
The hidden alphabets,
In the metaphysical scrolls,
In other histories of other worlds;
But for now he turns away

To the woman
Who kneels before him
As if the light hurt, streaming
Into the broken room, who kneels
Like a marble subject begging
For her child's life in the reign
Of Augustus. He wavers
As if a gulf had opened up beneath him
In the dusty floor;
He is silent, as if in honor of one
About to die in a Roman war;
He wavers in the air
Above the place where he had stood,
Then he becomes
One of the pictures of holy streams
That flow in Joseph's hoard of wood.

Mary lifts her face from the deep
Shadows burying the floor, as if Azrael
With his shovel suddenly
Had knocked the ceiling in, and says:
Then open our empty tombs as well
On each of us.

SOLDIER ASLEEP AT THE TOMB

Piero della Francesca

In Palestine,
Where you are counting stars
To stay awake,
There is a legend that
The world was built
From nothing. There is a plaster crack
Ascending through the air
Above your head,
And you have laid aside
Your headgear
Covered with wolf skin,
But don't sink back,
Don't let your head
Tilt back, don't look up toward
The heaven's starry gulf and close your eyes,
Because you must not fall
Asleep. You must not sleep—
In Rome they crucified a dog
And carried it across
The city crucified upon its cross
Because once, long ago,
A dog in his old age
Slept through his watch,
And as he slept, the Gauls
Hoisted themselves in multiplying
Shadows across the brick
You lean your head on here—

You dream you run your palm across
A wall, and then, because
You must not fall asleep, you study it:

A map of enigmatic bricks
They manufactured in a city
Not located on the map,
With a thousand-thousand roads of mortar
Branching and rebranching
And, smiling from a pike
Before the gateway to the palace,
The head of a beheaded wolf
Tiberius once held up by the ears
And claimed was Rome,
Somehow become
A cap of wolf skin
You've retrieved
And laid in a sack
To carry on your shoulder,
Headed for Palestine—

You toil through mortar streets
Between the bricks
As if you knew the way,
But really you must admit
You're lost. But really
You must not lose the way.

As for that trench
Stretching before you
You dare not set your foot into that pit——
Rome is dried mud scattered into an opened
Artery. You must not drop away.
But then you do, you step away . . .
You step into a desert
Stretching out beyond
The outer city curb of Rome
To Palestine, where you are counting stars
To stay awake,
Where a legend in this region says
The world was built from nothing,

But these colossal walls
Adorned with hoists and pulleys,
These wheels and ropes
Hanging from scaffoldings,
Transform the temple complex
Into siege towers they rolled up to the base
Of a wall where now you crumble
A little mortar in your palm,
No more than twenty grains,
Crushed out of lime, sand, straw, gravel,
Marveling as if it were all that was left
Of Rome——
Rome must have worn away
Behind this wall, buckled without a sound.
A bank of mud where someone

Plunged a torch and left a crater
Lit now by your torch,
A reservoir so vast an army drowns
Struggling to get across,
Racehorses floundering in shipwreck
Over flooded circus floors

Toward mass graves dug behind the Esquiline
For Pompey's elephants
Who pleaded for their lives,
For persecuted bears,
For waterspouts of birds
Slain on the sand floor of the arena
One piercing blue afternoon,
Now become merely a stench
Behind a supporting wall,

Though, like a room turned inside out,
The wall spills over,
A petrified waterfall
Of sludge from the ancient wars
They waged on animals,
And elephants are nudging you awake because
You must not sleep.
You lift your head. You are outside.
You cannot surrender
Your sense that there is still an outside
Outside.

But when you look out the corner
Of your eye, the heaps of
Flamingo carcasses the soldiers carry
On sagging litters,
As if they had done battle
With the sunset,
Become a heap of murdered angels
Pitchforked from a horrifying height.
You are afraid to look
To your right.
Outside, the world
Is a hurled object.
The world is a stone sphere
That has rolled through
Other lives, and as it grinds past,
It trails a red stream.
There is an atrocious
Implication here.
So you lower your head,
Keeping your eyes
Closed, as if that way nothing
Will be disclosed.
But you must not fall asleep,
Not even leaning on your shovel for a moment—

The world was built from nothing,
Not with the strewn
Abandoned trowels they used
For sealing off a crime,

Not with a general's
Unmentionable treasures
The soldiers were unloading
In a mountain range of spoils,
Not with mountains of lime,
Of sand, straw, gravel, while the god
Who made the world
Looked on in his foreboding—

But all through the empire
They built this same
Slipshod maze of rooms
Tilting on shallow foundations
You were digging
With a shovel
Below, in frightful terraces,
A brickwork complex hemmed in by
Several succeeding outer stairs
Rumored to lead outdoors
Just as you awoke because

You must not sleep, no matter what.
No matter how cold the nail
Embedded in the ice
Of three o'clock,
No matter who orders you to impale
The wolf's head you've been
Arrested with,
Alone, in man-made landscapes

Built with force, beneath
The creak of timber bridges,
And then that complicated falling down
Of nonexistent walls beneath
A watchtower whose foundation could
Equally have served
To hold a sanctuary up,

Where you take
A narrow hallway to the right,
Skirting the wall along a narrow passage
To reach the courtyard
Of—a palace like a marble mountain
In whose throne room you approach
Tiberius from behind his chair,
And he turns around—

There is an execution
At the heart of it.
Then several successive waves of terror,
As well as marble
From that island in the sea
Of Marmara, marble dust
Like the miraculous snowfall
In August delineating
The shape of the basilica:
A cruciform snowprint—
You lower yourself over the side,
To drop to the next terrace and run.

But each time you arrive here,
Lifting your lamp,
You hear a sound.
You know your orders, after all.
Yet when you put your eye
To a chink in the wall
And try not to inhale
The nauseating taste of mud

You see distant, underground
Fires pouring toward you
For miles and miles,
Underground walls buckling inward
On towering labyrinths,
And a native angel trundling
A dog he's saved
In a straw wagon with clattering
Wooden wheels,
A dog who gives a bark
And sticks his nose
Through wooden slats
Against the angel's hand,
And cages of crucifixions, one by one,
Swaying above the heads
Of a group of distant soldiers;
But you step back,

You dream you run your palm
Across the wall, you dream

You guard an empty place
Where the plaster-crack ascending
Through the air above your face
Has multiplied,
As if a force behind the wall
Were pressing toward you
From the other side.

ANGELS GRIEVING OVER THE DEAD CHRIST

The epitaphios of Thessaloniki

From those few famous silkworms smuggled
Into Constantinople in the head of a walking stick
Silk waterfalls
Poured from the ancient bolts

Into now-destitute reservoirs
Of church treasuries in Aachen,
In Liège, in Maastricht, in Sens,
In the Sancta Sanctorum of the Vatican,

Bright rivers seeping past
The age when a teaspoonful of
Silkworm eggs the size of one grain
Could endow a church,

The age when the letters in the words
Of sacred testaments were
Unreeled in the coastal cities of Asia Minor,
When a bookworm conspired

To wrest a maze of empty roads
Through the words *My Lord*—
That ancient, flickering text
Once permanently affixed

By blind but face-picturing, speechless
But law-breaking wooden shuttles,
Now a heap of gold wires displayed
With a crumbling silk vestment someone

Plucked from a shovelful of dust
During one of those treasure hunts conducted
In the burying grounds, in other eras,
A shovelful of dust

Now blowing into your eyes,
As if a storm wind from Paradise
Blew the rumors of this death
So hard you must cover your eyes

Before the museum case.
The late afternoon tugs
At a gold thread you can hear fraying
When you close your eyes,

A thread you feel your way along,
A thread at which the invisible globe pulls,
Leading you to the end of the world
Where there is a pile of

Clothes stolen from the grave,
Where your fear is relegated
To a masterwork of silk slaves—
That He is dead.

Here death is only a flash of worlds
Unfurled from a rifled
Church treasury, and you are invited
To walk this alluvial wave of gold,

To walk in the labyrinths
Of the angels' howls,
To run your hands along the walls
Of the silk thread's passageways,

To feel with your fingers
The angels' barbaric, stifled,
Glittering vowels
Tightly woven with gold wires.

If you were to tug at one,
Unraveling the angels
Into a vivid labyrinth of thread
From the fourteenth century

Backwards to the scissors blade
A seraph takes to a fragile
Filament of gilt
According to a law still unrevealed,

The shroud would disappear
In the gust of a little breeze
From this door left ajar
Into the next life,

The threshold we cross with closed eyes—
Where angels hide behind their backs
The saws with which they mean
To saw the present from the past,

Oblivious to the scarlet threads
That prove to be hidden among
The filaments, those red rivers
Running through the theme of time

So shockingly—so before you set foot there,
Take heed. This is the work
Of Byzantine silk slaves confined
To the palace grounds at Constantinople,

And you must beware.
There was a way station
On the Silk Road
Where the authorities executed

Traitors in a wooden box
In innumerable, unspeakable ways.
When you touch this shroud from the east
You take that hundred feet of road.

You must walk softly past.
You must try not to look.
The torrent of words—later, later.
Here tongues are cut out,

And that is why the howling
Is mute,
Gilded, herringboned.
Because although this is death,

It is the work of slaves
Whose task was only
To expose the maximum amount of gold thread
To the ceiling price of so many nomismata

Per square inch, in a swift mischief
Of curious knots, of mazes
Flashing past, of straight paths
Made inextricable,

So look again.
The angels wring their hands
Over a statue. They are deranged,
But not by grief. They mourn

Not a body, but a work in bronze.
They do not bring a mortal to the grave.
But we onlookers who grieve and grieve—
We cannot relegate this thought

To a glory woven cryptically
In heavy silks;
We cannot consign it, sweep it off,
For we cannot weigh

In our palms the empty cocoons,
We cannot study
Within the secret workshops
Of the silkworm,

We cannot touch the boiling
Water where the spools whirl,
We cannot learn firsthand
The bleakness of the craft

With which God made the world,
We cannot recount the legend that,
When they met face-to-face, both
God and the worm laughed.

CHRIST DEAD

Andrea Mantegna

1

Found among the painter's
Possessions at his death,
Something, of which one glimpse
Will wound your soul forever.

Something you seem to glimpse
Through intermediate planes of haze,
As if beyond overturned blocks
Of carved, square stone,
Something lying at rest,
Lying alone, even beyond
The nameless "uncarved block"—

As if you put your eye
To a chasm in the wall and beheld,
Through a caesura in the kingdom,
Through a space you cannot squeeze through,

The radiance of true exile
Where he lay in Sion a stumbling block
And a stone of offense, but here
Pictured in a perspective so narrow
You may only rest your forehead
On the ancient mortarwork
That holds you back from him.

So that, before this open tomb,
Pressing your face against the stone,
Seeing these lips that have touched
The bitter bread, halted
Before these wounded feet you cannot help
But reach for, as if you could
Take them in your hands,
You cannot refuse
To bow your head.

2

Andrea Mantegna meant this painting
For his own funerary monument,
To be placed by his heirs
At the foot of his coffin,
But instead, to pay his debts,
They sold it off
Into the ravenous inventory
Of Sigismondo, Cardinal Gonzaga.

Back and forth, each day
For twenty years,
He paced the avenue between his house
And the ducal palace in Mantua—
The great avenue superimposed
By the little path that lay
Before him, the path through his days
To the end of his life,

Past workshop squabbles
And troubled relations with patrons
And lawsuits and false accusations,
Past easels with resurrections set
In the shadow-gardens
Of suburban residences of great families,
And curious drawings of recently
Unearthed antiquities
Seized for the collections of princes,
And designs for fountains, and ornamental scrollworks
In silverpoint and black chalk,

And gold cautiously ground into a powder
Measured out for gilt highlights
Trembling in mantles
Of pink watered silk,
And paper shapes wrought with scissors
For marveling onlookers,
And commissions for portraits
Of noble persons with riverscapes
Winding beyond palace windows—

But always ahead of him,
At the end of the path, this open tomb
That was not his.
Always with him until he died,
This rectangle of canvas
Propped on an easel in his house
In the upstairs room

Where, on September 13, 1506,
"At eighteen hours of the clock,"
He left behind his debts and cares,
He turned his back a last time
On his room above the street,
And began to toil up the side
Of Golgotha,
Where the cross, looming above,
Was empty now. No one was there.
And at the very end he bent to leave

Christ Dead behind,
Propped at the foot of the cross
Of his last breath.

3

Behind the little funeral procession
Winding down the slippery path,
The Roman soldiers turned away,
Gathered themselves, and fell
Into formation on the road—
Though one man twisted to look back
Over his shoulder several times,
Struck by something he couldn't say.

When he returned to Rome,
He heavily climbed the stairs
To the second story, to the same
Room where he had lived.
He unburdened himself,
Laying his sack aside on the same floor,
Setting his helmet down on the same table.
And, looking down into the lane
Of his old neighborhood below his room,
With his eye pressed to the cleft
In the wall, he saw, for himself,
The world he'd pined for in the east
Just as it was before he'd left.

TIBERIUS LEARNS
OF THE RESURRECTION

Eusebius, The History of the Church, *II*, *11*

In a mock-Rome, built with bird cages,
The swallow was arrested for spying,
The pelican's beak was sawn off
For fishing a governor's pond without permission,

And a parrot, which made its entrance
In a covered basket, like a puppet-king
Carried in a litter who had recited
Upon his first glimpse of Rome

The lamentation of captivity
On behalf of those he had betrayed,
Now ignites into a dazzling green torch,
Crawling headfirst down

The wires against which, unfurling,
It momentarily crucifies itself,
Then folds into silence.
In a mock-Rome on the island,

The mirrors tilted against the corners
Of the ceiling are stifling,
Producing other worlds of angles
To spy on, showing, backwards

And forwards, an infinity
Of emperors, in a sequence of silvery rooms
Where the dagger-man leaps
But strikes someone else;

Where, strung up like withered cats
Who were executed for stalking
The talking birds from the thirty provinces
It is the Emperor's prerogative to strangle,

There are garlands for the Emperor,
The "Delight of the Human Race"——
Now nodding off, and sleep is a sheet of water
Glazing his troubled features. Tiberius

Dreams his face is carved onto
The front of a marble head,
Yet through his lowered eyes he sees
A little sparrow rolling toward his feet

A dry, round ball of straw——
His hand trembles outstretched before it,
For it may conceal the face of Drusus,
A faceless, featureless husk

Like a war trophy, a straw globe
Girdled with rope, a head with feathers
Where the mouth should be,
The mouth stuffed with mattress feathers

Owing to death by starvation, a head
Wrapped and sent to the Emperor
As proof of execution,
To whose lips he lowers his ear:

Man is a lamp that goes out when
I wave my hand. Man is a walking stick's
Ghostly supporter, following along.
Man is the victim of a wasp. A sack

Dragged to the Wailing Stairs and dropped.
A beggar's penny hurled into a well.
Something to wrap and bury in a hill.
Man is a madman clambering onto

The throne of Julius the God
At Augustalia, who picks up Caesar's crown
And puts it on his head, a crown
To crown the ruin of others with his own . . .

He tries to push it away,
But his bones weigh him down;
He sees his hand clatter down to his lap
Like a bone in an empty dish

And he cannot raise it; he tilts his head
And peers into a cistern, where,
Glinting at the bottom of a rumor,
Like a portrait of the Emperor,

An object's blinding brilliance
Makes him gasp himself awake before
The rim of, not a cistern, but
An orange blossom, offering not water

But an undrinkable perfume,
Like a pillow held to the face.
And mosquitoes float around his head
Forming soft, delicate, crazed

Letters in the air, writing his name,
Tiberius Julius Caesar Augustus,
A secret message of blame
He could crush into blood spots

If he could lift his hand.
Shoved around the island's boundaries,
The ocean's hurling-engines
Hurl bubbles into sand,

And banks of green-lit thunderheads
Are siege machines
Constructed in the Pax Romana,
Contraptions meant to terrify,

Lighting up a court of blue lizards
Like *agents provocateurs*
Pretending to cower among the frescoes
Of lemon trees

Though they are at the brink
Of showing their knives.
And a scribe
Is seated with his plume poised

Precisely on the last uttered letter,
A statue that writes,
These are my temples in your hearts,
These my fairest and abiding statues.

For those that are erected of stone,
If the judgment of posterity should turn
To hatred, are scorned
As sepulchres.

To be buried in one's own likeness
And image,
For a statue of one's self to be carried
By a slave through eternity,

A statue that crumbles, beginning with the face,
Into lime powder, to be carried
Past a flotilla of imperial barges,
Like water lilies, floating among

Courtiers, soldiers, scholars,
All of them corrupt. He climbs a mountainside,
Balding, bowlegged, to survey his quarries,
And a marble stairway, polished by flies,

Begins to revolve, a waterwheel
He is condemned to tread *in perpetua*,
Even when it crumbles beneath his steps
Into a flat ocean across which a slave

Walks toward him, whose lips are leprous
But he has bent to kiss . . .
His lips touch, inexplicably, flame.
A man laid in a new tomb,

Like a statue in the marble workshops,
But the eyes blindfolded,
The chin bound with gauze,
The statue of a god—of Tiberius,

Whose slaves carry statues of him
Down to the wharves, by the hundreds;
His features are multiplied in marble
A thousand times over, set afloat

On rafts, on ships, on imperial barges
Setting off, with carved blocks of marble,
Streaming past the rivers and ports
Into the open sea, the waterways

Filled with images
Of him, bound for marketplaces,
Temples, sacred crossroads,
Gardens, libraries,

His lips frozen, speechless among
The courtiers, the senators, the soldiers,
Unable to respond, to speak, to read
Aloud an inscription from which

His engraved name is stricken,
The marble face sheared off,
Exploding on the marble floor,
Or shipwrecked

In sand-laden winds,
In Egypt, where oceans are ponds,
In the reefs off Scylla,
In Greek underwater caves,

Where he somersaults slowly downward
Through an oceanic realm:
It is not the Roman custom
To condemn any man before

The accused meets the accuser
Face to face and has an opportunity
To defend himself
Against the charge.

He tries to lift his head,
A whited sepulchre
With his features; his stone hand
Lies across the scroll,

But where he had drawn a map
There is only a palsied star,
Like a wheel of knives wheeling
Toward him; he wrestles back

And starts awake. Nothing is there.
Mosquitoes softly float
Along a stone wall that conceals
A map embedded with borders of lightning,

And thunder rolls the sky away on wheels
Like a stone ceiling
Painted with clouds, but stone, stone.
Yet a god ascends through the worlds.

THE RESURRECTION

Piero della Francesca

In the 1550s a lantern maker, Marco, testified
That as a child he had "led Piero by the hand"
Through the streets of Borgo San Sepolcro.
Piero, blind, and following a child guide along

The chessboard of his native city's streets
To the Civic Palace, within the tumbled walls
Of the Town of the Holy Sepulchre. Piero, blind—
Who once, with earth imported from the Black Sea,

Had dusted pinhole pricks on tracing sheets,
To trace the *Dream of Constantine* on the wall,
And the serf who leaned against his shovel
Awaiting Helen's command to dig for the cross,

And Pilate, impassive, hooded in the Judgment Seat,
And the beautiful Jew who was tortured in a well—
Piero, white-gowned, a cataract prisoner, now
Shuffling, with outstretched hands, while far-off bales

Of straw, in fields ignited by the sunset,
Smolder behind him, setting a broken wall on fire.
The hem of a mantle of tree roots flames up
Like a patch of ancient sewing work littered

With those pearls for which Duke Federigo paid
A great price back in the old life, stitched
With silver leaf, in luminous embroiderings,
Lying tossed like a discarded shroud over

Kindling sticks in the hedge of thorns
The goldfinch once inhabited, her nest
A torch's head fallen from its stick
Beyond the curb of the marbly dream-town,

Where towers, knocked down across the countryside,
Half crumble like sugar-cube constructions
For a wedding, or dissolve like knocked-over
Buckets of sand for children's battlements—

For a city left behind in the wake of the earthquake
Of 1352, or the quake at Christ's death,
Since history is behind Piero now, and
The goldfinch is saved, circling ecstatically

Above Piero's head as he climbs a cement staircase
Step by step. *When you were young, you girded*
Yourself and walked wherever you would. But
When you are old, you will stretch forth

Your hands, and another will gird you,
And carry you where you would not go.
Halting in the streets of Holy Sepulchre,
Grown old in the town of his nativity,

Taken by the hand to the Civic Palace,
He stops at the site of *The Resurrection*,
And lifts his outstretched hand from Marco's shoulder,
As if he groped for the lip of a stone coffin

From antiquity set only inches away from where
The blind man appears to be staring in fright
Into God's face. Behind him the pink twinkle
Of twilight is a banner moist with one drop

Of Jewish blood; before him, the distant
Blue mountain of Purgatory. His fingertips touch
Only picture-shadowing earth from the Black Sea.
Once he could squint at *The Resurrection* through

An ever-smaller pinhole of light, like
A pinhole pecked for him by the finch's beak,
Through which he sifted powder for his drawings—
She whose nest had fallen when the mowers

Burned away the branches, she who had let
Piero approach, but only so far, and then
Warned him off with her gaze of terror,
When he would have bent on his knees in the grass

To stroke her anxious, silky head with
A fingertip, touching the scarlet cap
That stained it like a tiny, bloody drop,
But he'd backed away, not wanting to scare her—

But the pinhole he had peered through closed.
Now his shoes press against the plaster wall
Of blind old age, backed up by the empty place
Brick walls depict, where paint is a scent

That still could conjure the belfries of papier-mâché
He had painted for an important Duke,
A famous humanist he'd once depicted traveling
At twilight in a straw wagon with angels

Conversing in seraphic languages
Along the outskirts of a shining thunderstorm
Before the distant prospect of Rome-Jerusalem-Urbino.
Now he stands sightless with his empty hand

Outstretched at the rough edge of the sepulchre
Recently broken open, before which
Jesus has turned to Piero, holding out to him
Death's unraveled, pitiful bandages.

THE DREAM OF CONSTANTINE

Piero della Francesca

Long after the Messiah's men have entered
Every room in the city, and long after
Your government and seat of earthly power

Trudges far to the north, its army tents recentered
And sunk, like a meteor burned into the map,
This is the real end of the Roman Empire,

This storyless, this never-heard-of place
You find within, where there is only Constantine,
And vegetation, nudging the faces of boulders

. . . you saw rivers washing the very gates of the towns,
from the bend which leads the highway back toward Belgica,
you saw everything waste, uncultivated, neglected, silent,

shadowy—even military roads so broken that scarcely
half-filled, sometimes empty wagons cross them . . .
You gave us your whole life . . .

And there is a letter fallen out of the sky—
Through a window, far off in the distance,
They have drawn the dripping body of Maxentius

From the river and fixed his head on a pike,
To send it to Africa—but you dream an alphabet letter
Would shine beyond the borders of the New Rome, except

You had your men pry out and melt the bronze,
Leaving a chasm in the shape of a lightning-obliterated
Monogram, and there will come a time as well that,

Once you have laid your hands on the treasure
Of the nails that fastened His hands,
You will melt them into bridle bits and a helmet

And precious coins stamped with your portrait.
A letter fallen, a chunk of pediment, a stone
Carved from the fallen fragments of a dead moon

That turns out, when you examine it, to be
A meteor fragment with an engraved, ambiguous
Pockmark among other stones plunged into walled gardens

An empress studies in a miniature, circular
Hand mirror she holds over her shoulder, studying
Her hair, and the void at the heart of power

Where the senators don't speak Latin anymore,
Where barbarian horses clatter the cavalry stairs—
But when she turns around to look, Rome isn't there,

Only marble-carved studies of leaf-and-shadow
Floating above the entrance to gates
Long thought to be the handiwork of Greek slaves,

Crowned with orange blossom, and senators convene
To share their thoughts and turn to you,
But when you look through the gate you see

Nameless prisoners milling in a pig yard—
You lay down a law that the sacred precinct
May not be violated. No one may approach

The plot of ground you set aside, an orchard
Painted with bird cages for the Empress
And nightingales in flight and fountain jets

Raining parabolas of evaporating silver.
But as you approach, you see a figure
Strung up by the neck in the afterlife

Above the jawbone of an ass, clothes shredded,
While, in the background, Christ is beaten and bound.
The secret of the Empire was now disclosed:

That an emperor could be made elsewhere
Than at Rome. Other planets. Other laws.
Other hammers knock an alabaster sheet

Into a maze of cracks, a map of conquered districts,
New countries for the levying of the tax;
Other shovels are striking at an urn marked,

In the simplest imperial style, simply "Bones."
Your bones, Constantine, for in the end nothing
Could save you. But as for one's death, fixed into

The future like a stone that cries out in a wall,
It isn't now in any case, not at this moment.
There are churches to build, with spirits drawing

Compass points in the dust only steps ahead
Of Constantine, and letters to write to Jerusalem:
We wish this church to be the most beautiful in the world.

We have issued instructions to that effect
To the Vicarius Orientis, and the Governor of Palestine.
You awaken, in a tent on a field of battle.

Though your men boil grass to drink the water,
Though the moon flickers out—the battle is over
Long after the Messiah's men have entered

Every room in the city, and long after
Your engineers have affixed a pentacle
To the city and reported rumors of its miraculous

Founding, long after the dedicatory mosaic,
The visual liturgy, the setting for a crisis
In gold glass, monophysite particles swimming upward

Out of the prisons of ecclesiastical geography,
Escaping when everything must be included,
Escaping when nothing must escape, not even dust,

For history is either a prison, a repository belonging
To the victorious Emperor, or else a patch of snow
A group of kneeling slaves hammers and hammers—

Let them hammer the heads of their own shadows.
You will win the battle. The city of Rome is yours,
And never mind the rumors thronging your ears

Like angels pouring along a map of black roads
Through the mosaic's gold squares, angels rushing
Toward you through the labyrinths of mortar

From other capitals with other crucifixions
At the ends of other lanes, dimly beheld
In cities that have yet to be founded,

At whose outskirts other emperors sleep in their tents.
For now there is you at the picture's center.
And never mind the angels thronging your ears

With rumors of lamps up ahead that refuse
To stay lit for your armies, with rumors
That no lamps are lit in the cities your armies enter.

PART THREE

A

MONUMENT

IN UTOPIA

A MONUMENT IN UTOPIA

(Osip Mandelstam)

When a word is spoken in the name

of its speaker, his lips move in the grave.

—TALMUD, TRACTAT YEVAMOT, 97A

1

In a time when poetry will be filled
With a peripheral fleet of swans
Glimpsed in the heavy, carved mirrors
That bring the willow park
With its long, statue-ringed, green ponds
Through the windowpane
Into the drawing room
So that, even standing inside,
We seem to look outdoors
Into a room of green rain;

In a time when poetry will no longer
Be a door fallen open upon
A dangerous conversation,
A door pushed shut in the Iron Age
Upon topics better saved for the open streets
And that famous glance
Over the shoulder,

Topics gliding over your life and mine,
But lighting upon the destiny of one
Who escaped to Paris;
In a time when, once having spoken,

A man will be allowed
Simply to resume growing older;

Then a notebook may be allowed to lie
Abandoned on the outer stairway,
Its pages turning freely back and forth
In the breeze, as if a spirit were reading,

And winter will come
Together with headlines in the *Herald*
Announcing that this season
Everyone in the city is mad for pearls,

Then a lost world will be only as trivial
And only as panic-engendering
As a lost pearl
That has rolled under the bed,
And, like all domestic artifacts
In this age, will be easily retrieved again—
Then the word *impearled*
Will no longer give way to the word *imperiled*,
Not even for you, who disdained to twist
Rhymes apart with a knife for their pearls—

And through the streets of the city, the cold pink cliff
Of afternoon's glacier will press its path,
Dropping at its forefront the crumbling
Particles of twilight's mauve, pushing past
The momentarily lustrous *glass panes*
Of eternity where you had laid
The humid whorls of childhood's breath.

No one will be under arrest;
The enlightenment will be behind us;
When we hurry past the metropolitan library
No one will look out at us in fright
From the top of his cast-off overcoat,
No one will reach from his orphan's sleeve
With a child's yearning hand
Trapped in the rising waters of the age,
No features hauntingly difficult to place
Will perch precariously on a throat
As gaunt as a starved pencil.
And the vexing labyrinths
Of injury and debt will have plunged away
Together with the false testimony of
Bad neighbors and ungrateful friends;
No one will scrawl a message that ends
If I can just get through these years . . .

And surging away, far behind us,
That purge of down-at-the-heels cosmopolitans
Will be swallowed up
Together with our recollection
That these mammoth canals
And cavernous buildings were built
With the labor of prisoners like you
Back when the uprisings meant
That men rose up to dispose
Of their next-door neighbors.

Even if the avenues will be mobbed
With former prisoners from that time,
A non-person will be free to survive the winter,
To observe, from the comfort of his own coat,
His native city by lamplight
Along the black ice of the frozen river,
With its frilly crust
Of half-lit, golden snow
Like a mille-feuilles
Glimmering with apricot glaze
And ready to crumble beneath the tooth,
Whose sugar grains melt on his tongue——

He will be free to look into a succession
Of snowflakes poised on his glove
As if he had idly lifted a kaleidoscope
To his eye and seen street maps
Of harmless utopias succeed one another
In a swift, geometrical blaze,
Like hypothetical maps
Of a village you once passed through,
Though functionaries have made a point
Of sealing off those documents
That mention you.

Back then, the heavenly axle tree,
Like that verse about the sound the earth makes
As it rotates on its invisible axis
In a breathless rhyme with your name,

Was only a set of revolving doors
Swooping into a marble office building,
Constructed and installed
By means left unrecorded,
Where a malicious servant of the state—
Who, after all, was a non-person too,
Whose teeth doubtless pained him,
Whose backstairs doubtless smelled of ammonia—
Was seated at his desk in 1937,
Before seventy speeches, a blizzard of papers,
Correspondence witnessed under
Dread of death, and documents leading to a man
Pushing a wheelbarrow of stones
Along a path near Vladivostok, as if
Illustrating an axiom as yet unpropounded.
He blotted with a tissue the fresh ink
Where his signature stained the document,
Tamping his name, as if he tried to arrest
A seepage of blood:

A sphere has squeezed itself into my room,
Backing me against the wall of my office——

What is it! The New World escaped from a pen,
The substitute world we designed

To put an end to suffering and doubt,
Though once it did loll and roll about

Above the most poverty-stricken and threaten
To explode——soap!——

A hollow, wobbling, flashing sphere
But not this hardened monoglobe

Rolling out of the palace
Of the nineteenth century

I thought the ages rolled away from us
Not toward us

I first heard it
Rolling through a word,

A word like a bubble fleeing,
But a bubble growing

Until it rolls through the streets, it rolls up
To the door of my office and squeezes through——

Oh, the world is rounder in Red Square
Than it is anywhere—

If I slash it with my scissors,
I see my shadow on its surface

If I stab it with my pen,
If I take a hammer to it—but the stains,

If it should burst, the horrid stains,
Oh, worlds, worlds are dashing in my brains!

2

Even if war should rattle
That window on Europe again
Beyond the mahogany dining table
Shined into a dark-brown mirror,
The silver inkwell picked up at an auction
Gleams on its stand
Like an ornate wishing well,
A well no longer brimming
With the ice-crowned black water
Toward which the Grand Princes were lowered,
But only with a spray of heavy roses
Sipping transparent water,

An inkwell that once belonged
To Victor Hugo,
Who, as he lifted and stroked
His beard like a mantle of
Century-old wisteria, had declared
That torture was at an end
Around the world, and had raised
His glass to that thought—

Even if war should rattle that window again,
Now the fall
Of the Second Empire is no more
Momentous than currency changing hands
At a distant border, though
Mixed with some reports of war,

And rumors of revolution mean
Only that there will be time
For uninterrupted study
At the once desolate kingdom
Of your desk, where you may escape
Everything and everybody,
Where the only thing you surrender to
Is a paper world, where error may be rectified
With a single pencil stroke
And no one is hurt,
Where among the reams of blank paper,
And the rules of the pencil
With its featureless, annihilating eraser,
You are at liberty to lower your ear
To the verse of an ancient eclogue

Where the house of the bee
Is enlarged by another room,
Held fast with fragrant wax,
And, nearer and nearer,
The humming workers thresh the air
Charged with their labor's mysterious joy,

And snails sway on little stems,
Lost in a meditative slumber
As morning opens up a box
Of heavenly blessings without number.
You hear a girl's foaming hems

Churn a wake of white, blue-eyed grasses—
She carries her flower scissors open
To shear the locks
Of the heaped-up lilac branches
Leaning like tinted sheep
Against a fence that sags beyond repair,
As a cream-yellow, infant cabbage moth
Blunders into her hair—

You could reach your hand
Into the tendrils along the nape
Of the sweet peas exhaling on the trellis,
Of the rose mallow, the may apple, the fox grape,
In the century of carelessness at piano lessons,
Of embroidered alphabet letters,
Of paper prisons for crickets,
Of pulling wooden swans on strings—
Of coming face-to-face with
The surprising beetle at the foot
Of the blade of grass, whose mandibles
Revolve at the foundations
Of your memory,

Until the only revolution
You can follow any longer
Is day revolving into night, as silently
As leaves alternating with shadows
In black and white on a balcony—nothing more,

And rumors mean only that you seize
The chance to abandon your book,
Though successive new worlds roll
With a great force over the floors
Of your era, staining our ceilings
In that apartment where we still are frozen,
Where we still flash our eyes
Past the lists of the accused,
We still find our families' names
Scribbled into the margins
In an unfamiliar hand—
Where, even without you, we still stand
At the window and stare *into the frost's face.*

But you loved the winter because it was
"The one thing they could not take away"
Even after that night the end appeared
As a broken window, after the war
That landed on the wall of your apartment
Like a falling star—except
That apartment had only ever existed on paper,
And paper was the first thing
They would take away.

3

And that bookcase from your childhood—
Never to be recovered, of course—
That bookcase your parents moved
From one apartment to the next,
From Maximilian Lane to
Ofitserskaja Street and Zagorodnyj Prospekt,
The one you saved, and saved, and saved,
And *then* lost

As you fled the ravine that opened up
Between two revolutions
While families peeped from basement windows
Along one of those black boulevards
We see in the peripheries of
A glass of boiled water
At whose rim you sniffed the lead pipes
Of waterworks from the Golden Age—

Your childhood encyclopedia
With those names that had not yet begun
To boil on the maps,
And the gilt-edged Bible's
Whiff of smoking Paradise
Among the gutted Hebrew letters,

And the flattened hemispheres
With the seven blue oceans
You had thumbed threadbare,
Your schoolboy Herzen

With your scribbled drawing
Of a man seated at the base of the "wall
Which cannot be destroyed,"

Your Hans Christian Andersen's
Nightingale, where there is a courtier
Of such importance that, when a man
Of lower rank dares to ask him a question,
He habitually answers only "P,"
Which means nothing at all;

And Baudelaire, Hugo, Lamartine,
The choices of a French governess,
And notebooks where everything
You penciled into the margins has smeared
Like the pain-blunted words you searched for—
Supposedly easily retrieved—
In the throbbing labyrinths
Of a cigarette ember, in the remotest
Reaches of migraine, the margins
Where you had copied out
Something from Aristotle, because he broke

Words into syllables,
Then into letters: the word PERSON,
If it was broken into P and E and R,
Still would shed no blood, would expose
Nothing that would make us dizzy.
Beyond the disintegration of a word

A string of letters simply floats away—
And beyond the disintegration of a letter
There floats a silence so absolute
That, presumably, there is nothing left to say,

Not even in your turn-of-the-century
"Illegally suppressed"
Editions that weighed so much
They bowed the shelf and it threatened to snap,
The way other bookshelves in other countries
Have sagged with an additional fact
Since the date of your arrest.

4

Those books, dumped out,
Are still drifting down somewhere between
The autumn of 1900
And the later fortunes of a region
That hurled itself into a terrifying dream;
They still are falling through the air,
Still fluttering out across the century
And have not hit bottom,

Nor has that trunkful
Of worthless paper money
From the time of Nicholas the Second—
Pathetic money, stuffed behind
Miniature embroideries of your native city's
Colossal neoclassical boulevards
Built with forced labor
And depicted on frivolous cushions;

Money, shaken from the pages of novels,
Fluttering down through the air of an apartment
Where papers are sewn into pillows,
Or into the linings of coats,
Or stuffed into shoes,

With papers that fluttered out of your sleeve
On the night of your arrest,
And drifted over Europe,
Landing here, on a library shelf;

Money, no longer stamped, like the odes
From that period, with the cheap,
Benevolent portraits of monsters,
No longer giving off an acrid scent
As if a frightened man had touched it,
No longer with torn edges unraveled
Into a plush hedge the chief police interrogator
Runs his thumb along, before he crumples the bills
One by one into paper spheres, and wades
Among skittering ghost-worlds,
On his way out the door, his ankles
Brushing against wads of paper
That once upon a time
Could have bought you a coat.

Five thousand miles east of *childless Petrograd*,
You! You, with your hair-raising tales,
Your coat without buttons, your raging fits,
Your history of poverty, your torn cigarettes!
You, with your heart still set
On impossible things,
Touching the top of your head absently
Like the Pharaoh's baker trying to explain
His dream that there were birds
Devouring cakes from a basket on his head—
Then falling silent to feast upon a grain of sugar
That audibly melted on your tongue,
A crumb you lifted to your lips
With a delicate finger-and-thumb
In a trance of concentration,
The first grain from that half kilo of sugar
Like a sack of diamonds finely ground
For which you traded a shredded
Yellow leather overcoat in December,
Though God knows where you'd acquired
Such a coat,

Though granted that, in the old stories,
Garments are lavished on paupers;
Granted that, in one's childhood books,
The coat of the king
Always comes to rest around
The stooped shoulders of his poorest subject,
Albeit no longer lined with a flash of silk,

No longer even held together
With the precious stitches of silk thread

Inside the coat of Akaky Akakevich,
Who, though he squandered all that he had
For his lofty dream of a new overcoat,
Though for months he went hungry at night,
Though he did without tea and candles,
Still had to skimp on the calico lining
And a collar of cat's fur.

Even at the Expulsion, God made
With His own hands garments of fur and skin
For the expelled—

But for you the sum of your inheritance,
Of which you were robbed anyway,
Was a veil of threads handed down
Through the generations, a veil descended
From that succession of stolen overcoats
Stuffed with paper shreds
From the nineteenth century.

Out there a giant scissors pursues
Little men, insignificant men, non-persons,
Up and down the lanes of Vtoraya Rechka,
Clacking and clacking behind them,
Cutting their overcoats into streamers,
Until all that is left is a bit to drape

Over the shoulders, but not enough
To cover the face with, when the time comes.

And who wouldn't want to press
His coat on you?
Who wouldn't exchange
Your bunk for his comfortable bed?

Who, then, that has lived such a life
Has escaped the Emperor's notice?
For each and every one of them
Was denounced.
What land and sea did he not thoroughly search,
What clefts in the rocks,
What secret holes in the earth,
That he might bring to the light of day
One who was hidden there? And once he had found
Such a one, he would carry him away,
And not to his palace, either.

6

You will be free to wander
In the metropolitan library,
Free to stare,
Without arousing suspicion,
At the statue voted by the senate
To honor Poetry,
Once a block of undifferentiated marble
Originally destined, in the old life,
For a grandiloquent hotel lobby
In the Empire style, hinting at transports
Of stone in wobbling wheelbarrows driven
Along filthy lanes by men whose fingernails
Are suitable for decapitating fleas
And scratching their beards as if
They sandpapered a shadow—
Once a block of marble,
Yet now a spirit glinting in the room,
With a starry hoard of words
Like tiny prisms on its lips.

Although the rhapsodes themselves
Will be banished from the reading rooms
To the public park, exiles
Even from the reconstructed life,
Framed in the library's windows,
They will reappear in bronze
Along the radiating paths,
Among the avenues of limes, for miles;
They will populate the gravel walks

In greatcoats, holding hats and books,
Although with interchangeable heads
In deference to changing tastes and styles.
Among the reveries of oval ponds
Like looking-glasses with drifting swans,
None will be represented pushing a wheelbarrow,
No man, with his head between his knees,
Will be seated and puking between his feet,
No scarecrow with his hands
Fastened beneath his armpits,
Looking cautiously over his shoulder
From his gravel mound,
Will thus indicate the wind-chill factor
On the "date of death unknown."

Seated in the shade of your monument,
Where you will wear an absurd morning coat
Far above your station in life,
Schoolboys will read your lines:
Now I'm dead in the grave with my lips moving
And every schoolboy repeating the words by heart.
Although you are laid nowhere in a grave,
Although you speak without moving your lips,
Although your words shine by themselves.

Beyond the statues of Important Persons
Posthumously rehabilitated,
Retired prison guards will be seated in the shade
In flocks along the banks of a green river

As if a goosegirl had driven
Them to the edge of the pond.
Seated on stone benches,
They will be excused, and pensioned off;
In their eighties now, they will snooze
And nurse their tea, and their frail shoulders
Will shake when they cough.
At night, for them, there will be
A tincture of valerian and a teaspoon
Glimmering on the bedside table.

Even that one will have attained
A gentle expression
Who stirred the gravel with a stick
And asked, *So now where is your poetry?*
Even his shadow will tower over nothing more
Than a board of dominoes,
His double chin propped on his fist,
His elbow crushing wadded headlines.

He will die in his own bed
Like an old woman, his head dropping down
Between his glass of tea and a needlepoint cushion
Where a tattered finch flutters,
Though it is stabbed to the heart,
Across a shallow autumnal stream
Plush with once-bright-red thread
Gone muddy brown;

For him, death will lie
Open like a newspaper in a dream,
A paper he ransacks his apartment for,
And when he lays his hands on it at last,
As he smooths the crinkled page to read,
He will simply spread before his face
Not a page but, oddly, a black comet,
Or rather a rococo ornament in empty space
Hanging intriguingly before his eyes,

And he will turn his face toward an evening
So thick with butterflies
Along a blurry road
That the convoy truck in which he is transported
Will lay two black tire stripes
Through the white, rustling millions . . .

It will have evaporated,
That whiff of the scaffold, the siege tower,
Of vaults sealed so long that no one
Would wish to break them,
That sense that a bone is being broken
Somewhere in the world,
That one's number is called out.

Even the dictator, the son of a devout
Washerwoman and a cobbler who savagely beat him,
Will be seated in the library among
Unsuspecting readers,

Including you, where you will be hidden
Behind your book, thumbing the last page
Of your life, still afraid to read it;

Even the dictator will leave off
Doodling wolves in red ink,
And will begin, tentatively, to explore
The vaults of white paper
With a sharpened pencil,
Where howls still will be trapped
In the gray zone of lead;
Even he will turn a sequence of the intricate
Misfortunes of other people
Into icy, twinkling, jagged meters
Until the page will be as blackened
As those black wells
Into which you were lowered
In a nightmare of the skull-piled woods
Outside of Novgorod:

The world is a closed and unique system,
A monoglobe, a monument to permanence,
With one center and a limited circumference,
A manifest point to exile others from,

To banish the vanishing point once and for all,
After we've swept the past into it and shut
The lid. There is no point outside the world
Which cannot be destroyed. And the world is small—

We may measure it, in inches, with calipers,
On a sheet of paper, and calculate its weight.
We may whirl the pencil around and around
The needle that bores a hole in the paper's center

Into the lives of others. There are no others;
Others are us; and we have covered sinkholes
And graves and regions of war with paper
On which it is written and signed that we are brothers:

Here history begins. As for that creature
Cowering in the corner, he is one we found
On the other side of the paper wall
When we began to bore a hole in the world—

Pay no attention. We approach the hour
Without populations of rebels, without synagogues
Of doodling devils, there will be no jails
Once we have emptied them and we will scour

The prison walls before we close them forever.
No matter what blood spattered on our shoes,
Whatever lives lie crumpled at our feet,
We'll roll the globe before us with a lever,

We'll prove beyond a doubt the world is man's,
A monument to us, a monoglobe
With a manifest point and a limited circumference,
And it never can fall into the wrong hands.

If I could begin again,
Time is something I would measure
In the generations of roses, evolving across
Gulfs we have no records of,
Eons without archives,
Eras without witnesses,
Without surviving portraits,

Roses flowering past the cliffs
Of thirty million years
Without intent,
In galaxies of tints,
In repetitious, variegated depths
Above the sinkholes of our wars,
Our vanishing points,
With hints
Portrayed in velvet;

If I could begin again,
I would measure time in the generations of
Roses, and not the succession
Of rulers of men,

In that fragrant clambering
Across the cliffs between millennia,
In the world without us,
Roses linking their chains among outcroppings
Of stone and shale
High overhead or drifting

To the bottom of twenty dozen centuries
Or oversprawling, on their jagged stems,
Chaos—

To never wonder what they meant,
To never envision
Nero's face again,
Though roses were destined
To be his favorites,
Fluttering from his ceiling,
One of the varieties of damask rose
Killed off, they say,
By the eruption at Pompeii,
Depicted on the walls of plastered bricks,
Unscented as music, and
The gallica roses, established
After the fall of Rome wherever
They had fallen,
They never asked themselves
Whether it was worthwhile
To save the Roman Empire
In order to make it a vast prison
For scores of millions of men.

Though here
The Latin library crumbles,
The archives tumble, the Tabularium
Buckles into a rose garden
Where we piled texts from centuries

In cliffs of commentaries
While nature was tracing out her beauties
In the medium of flower-flesh,
Building her roadways
Out of haze,
Her repositories out of snow
Whether thirty million years ago
Or here and now

Where the year of your death
Rolls up to the foot
Of Stalin as if he could give orders
For the years to come and go,
As if he could decree
That not a single green leaf
Is to be left on the branches,
That each growing leaf
From the old world
Is to be repressed,
Nothing is to be left,
Though his secretary
Will scissor roses away
To set on the great man's desk,
In Utopia, when he will rest from his wars—

But there, where roses press ahead,
There the boundaries are vague,
The numbers of their species
Are disputed, each new leaf

Unfurls and grows
In time's sidereal gulfs
Toward other flowerings,
Other unfurlings, other
Floatings toward a very different future
Rose by rose,
Flowering above
Brick walls whose foundations
Are shattered statues
Wedged into the foundations of bad dreams
Our flashlights scan,
A jumbled perpetual night of broken pieces,
Of frozen motion and sagging seams,
Pressing through a rift in time,

Flowering past that mound of heads
At Utopia's borders,
Composed of portraits of
The heads of households,
Of beloved daughters, blind rhapsodists,
Of gods reduced to begging with
Their delicate hands held out midair,
Marble arms and legs akimbo in frozen rape,
Masterpieces ground down for ballast,

Even when we pass the torch
Of our holocaust near their petals,
They instantly parch into irretrievable
Miniature scrolls we cannot excavate,

A speechlessness
With nothing to lament,
Uttering nothing even for the one
Whose face we know
Amid the blind roots of trees
In an apple orchard, in the loam
Of centuries of rubbish, jammed up
To the hilt in mud and snow,
In the generations
Of roses flowering past a group of graves
We have never visited,
Graves we haven't known of,

Above which pink-golds, rose-golds, gold-reds
Are evolving, with nothing in mind,
The tints that make their way
So wordlessly, millions
Mutating into vermilions, flowering past
The established *annus mundi*
Written into rock
In 49 at Antioch,
At Gaza in 61,
At Alexandria in 30,
Bostra in 106—

Clambering past borders
And successions of years, with
Multileveled, multipetaled realities
Reaching beyond our eventual absences

For resurrections expressed without
Faith or doubt,
Compared to which our lives and histories,
Our moral wanderings,
The history of our disgrace,
Are merely a crumpled disorder
To shovel over,

Merely pages to tear from
Childhood's classic picture books,
Where, among the formal gardens,
The little figures of Redouté and Josephine
Bend to the easels:

He is teaching the art of flower painting
To a queen
To celebrate their bloodless beheadings,
And at their backs
Bushels of roses heaped along the fence
Disappear along hazy roads
In districts we no longer stroll,
Among what overgrowings,
What loiterings on trellises,
What comings and goings
In other people's childhoods,

The roses' silence unbroken,
Piled high in wagons like
Captives bound for the metropolis,

Trundling past each century,
The favorites of Nero,
The possessions of Constantine,
The emblems of Saladin,
Flowering toward a time when there is no
Nero, no anti-Nero,
No Constantine, no Saladin,
But only roses on their paths
To someplace else,
Some other point of rest,

Flowering past our multitudes
Of local eras, our eschatologies,
Our beginnings and ends,
Our indictions, our "destinies of kingdoms,"
Our fifteen-year cycles, our holy days
And warring calendars,
Our Era of Martyrs,

Flowering past the fence
Above our death dates hidden even
From the angels—
Transitory monuments
Pouring out their whorls,
Piling up their treasure heedlessly
In the vaults of air.

NOTES

✺

THE LAMPLIT ANSWER

KREMLIN OF SMOKE

The twenty-year-old Chopin was visiting Stuttgart when he heard that Warsaw had fallen to the Russians; his journal entry for that night accuses God of being a Russian. Chopin never returned to Warsaw.

Several details in this fictional portrait, such as Chopin's gift for mimicry, his mother's love of Rousseau, and the eccentric dress of his childhood piano teacher, are drawn from Chopin's letters and journals and from Adam Zamoyski's biography, *Chopin*.

THE SELF-PORTRAIT OF IVAN GENERALIĆ

Generalić addresses his wife, who had died in the same year that he painted this self-portrait.

IMAGINARY PRISONS

The title is a translation of *Carceri d'Invenzione*, G. Battista Piranesi's series of engravings of fantastical prisons, which was published in Rome *c.* 1760.

THE HEAVENLY FEAST

Simone Weil died in August 1943, in a sanatorium in Ashford, Kent, England. Several years after her death, an epitaph in Italian was placed anonymously on her grave. It translates: "My solitude has held in its grasp the grief of others until my death."

A GILDED LAPSE OF TIME

PART ONE/A GILDED LAPSE OF TIME

Phrases from Dante's *Comedy* are drawn variously from translations by John Ciardi (New York: Mentor, 1970), Allen Mandelbaum (New York: Bantam, 1984), and John D. Sinclair (Oxford: Oxford University Press, 1939).

Phrases from St. Augustine's *Confessions* are taken from translations by R. S. Pine-Coffin (Baltimore: Penguin, 1961), Rex Warner (New York: New American Library, Mentor-Omega, 1963), and Eugene TeSelle in "Augustine," in *An Introduction to the Medieval Mystics*, edited by Paul Szarmach (Albany: State University of New York Press, 1984).

when you hear your name: This is an adaptation of a folk superstition described by Nikolai Gogol, in *Old-World Landowners,* as a prophecy of one's own imminent death.

bees who laid aside: In Isaiah 7:18–19, following the prophecy of the Messiah, God whistles for the bees to come out of the land of Assyria.

unfinished combs: In I Samuel 14:24–29, the Israelites are faint with hunger, and in the woods they have found a honeycomb that drips on the ground; but Saul has forbidden them to eat. Only Jonathan has not heard his father's interdiction: "wherefore he put forth the end of the rod that was in his hand, and dipped it in an honeycomb, and put his hand to his mouth: and his eyes were enlightened."

In classical antiquity, bees and honey were associated with poets and poetry-making, as in Plato's *Ion,* and with gifts of divination, prophecy, song, eloquence, and truth-telling. Bees were thought to embody the souls of the dead, as in Aeneas' vision of underworld souls destined for reincarnation in the *Aeneid,* VI, 703; it was thought they could impart gifts of poetry to those whose lips they touched with honey, as in the epitaph by Antipater of Sidon on Pindar in the *Greek Anthology,* VII, 34, and in some instances the bees were said even to have built a honeycomb on the poet's mouth. In Latin poetry, this legend frequently is expressed explicitly, for example, in Horace's "Ego apis Matinae," and implicitly, for example, in Virgil's associating of Orpheus with Aristaeus, the first beekeeper, in Book IV of the *Georgics.*

2

God repented after He made man: Genesis 6:6: "And it repented the Lord that he had made man on the earth, and it grieved him at his heart."

those vessels God had wanted to use: The "breaking of the vessels," also known as "the death of the primordial kings," is a kabalistic Jewish creation legend, suggested in the Zohar and famously elaborated by Isaac Luria. The version of the legend quoted here is recounted by Gershom Scholem in an essay entitled "Sin and Punishment."

In the *Trattatello in laude di Dante,* Boccaccio, on the authority of Dante's friend Piero di Giardino, writes that Dante had hidden away the last thirteen cantos of *Paradiso* before embarking on a journey to Venice that proved fatal to him. After his sudden death, the ending of *Paradiso* was considered lost. Dante's sons attempted to finish the poem themselves. Eight months after Dante's death, his son Jacopo dreamed that Dante appeared to him and led him to the room where the last cantos were hidden behind a mat pasted to the wall next to the bed where Dante had died. When Jacopo awakened from the dream, he hurried to the house of Piero di Giardino to rouse him, and the two men hastened to the room where Dante had died; there they discovered the cantos in the location described in the dream. The verses were in a dangerously deteriorated condition from the damp mold of the wall, but they still were legible enough for Jacopo to make a copy of them.

4

The fountains also of the deep . . . : Genesis 7:11 et seq.

6

We are water: II Samuel 14:14: "We are like water that is spilt on the ground."

7

The speculation that the concentric spheres must exist is quoted from Theon of Smyrna, *Expositio rerum mathematicarum ad legendum Platonem utilium,* translated by S. Sambursky in *The Physical World of Late Antiquity* (Princeton: Princeton University Press, 1962).

8

There is no depiction of God the Father in the mosaics in San Vitale, except for the image of the divine hand reaching down from heaven to withhold Abraham's hand from the sacrifice of Isaac. The Messiah is portrayed both as a beardless youth enthroned on a celestial sphere in the apse, from which the four mystical rivers pour, and as the risen Redeemer in a medallion at the center of the interior vault leading toward the apse.

10

the creation was subjected: Paul writes "the creation was subjected to vanity" in Romans 8:20.

marble caterpillars: In *Purgatory,* X, 124–26, Dante describes the human soul:

> . . . *do you not know that we are worms and born*
> *to form the angelic butterfly that soars,*
> *without defences, to confront His judgement?*

(TR. A. MANDELBAUM)

a holy stream: Circulating throughout the *Comedy* are numerous metaphors portraying God as a miraculous source of water, a fountain, a river, a spring, an ocean, a heavenly raining. In *Paradiso,* XXX, 88–89, Dante dips his face into a river of light and lets it cascade from his eyelashes. Dante is thought to have died of a malarial fever he contracted in the marshlands between Ravenna and Venice.

Ephphatha: In Mark 7:34, Jesus utters the untranslated Hebrew word *Ephphatha* in healing a man of two ailments simultaneously: deafness and impaired speech.

The authenticity of Dante's death mask, which was not discovered until centuries after his death, is disputed.

That wound, inflicted inadvertently: In Canto XIII of the *Inferno*, in the Wood of the Suicides, Dante is struck dumb with pity and fear when, at Virgil's urging, he hesitantly tears a little branch away from a thorn tree and the tree shrieks in pain; words and blood issue out simultaneously. Dante discovers, in this terrible way, that the thorn trees in this desolate wood are the transformed souls of human suicides, who are enabled to speak only in the medium of blood, and only as a result of injury. Dante draws this moment from a similar incident between Aeneas and the soul of Polydorus in the *Aeneid*.

A bell at the Dante Museum in Ravenna, next to Dante's Tomb, rings thirteen times at dusk in memory of Dante's homesick recollection of the Compline bell in *Purgatory*, VIII, 1–6.

Whose movement is swift . . . : In *Convivio*, II, iii; and Dante's speculation that without the movement of the primum mobile the planet Saturn would be hidden from earth for fourteen and a half years, the planet Jupiter for six, and the planet Mars for nearly a year, is recorded in *Convivio*, II, xiv, translated by Patrick Boyde in *Dante Philomythes and Philosopher* (New York: Cambridge University Press, 1981).

She had lived: Dante's astronomical calculation of the length of Beatrice's life is recorded in *La Vita Nuova*, I, ii, translated by Barbara Reynolds (New York: Penguin, 1969).

to fix it in my sight: As he approaches the brilliant Sphere of the Sun, Dante asks the reader to "lift your eyes with me to see the high wheels," as translated by Allen Mandelbaum, or to "raise your eyes across the starry sphere," as translated by John Ciardi, in *Paradiso*, X, 7–8, in order to regard the point of the vernal equinox as the mark of the perfection of God's art; and he says in line 12 of the same canto that this is a picture which God, out of love, has "fixed forever in His sight" (tr. Ciardi).

ANNUNCIATION
2

The ambitious building activities of Herod the Great, who rebuilt the Second Temple, are described by Josephus in *The Jewish War*, I, 401.

4

Some details of the capture of the people in the first stanza are taken both from Thucydides' description of the captured Athenians in Sicily in *The Peloponnesian War* and from Josephus' description of the destruction of Jerusalem in *The Jewish War*.

5

The description of the end of days in lines 4–7 is from Ecclesiastes 12:3–7.

All the knives were reground . . . : Adapted from rules, in the Babylonian Talmud, Tractat Avodah Zarah, 49b and 76b, concerning the purification of knives and the destruction of pottery (in fulfilling the requirements of kashrut), and the destruction of fabric woven with implements made from wood associated with idols.

6

Suetonius reports in *Augustus*, XCI, that once a year Augustus would sit before his house on the Palatine, with his hand outstretched, begging for coins, in obeyance of a dream he had once had.

SOLDIER ASLEEP AT THE TOMB

The portrait of the sleeping soldier who faces the viewer in Piero della Francesca's *Resurrection* (c. 1458) in the Civic Palace at Borgo San Sepolcro is said, by Vasari, to be Piero's self-portrait.

Livy recounts in his *History of Rome*, V, xlvii, the legend of the Gauls' assault "one starlit night" on the Capitoline. The Gauls climbed the walls so silently that the watchdogs were not awakened, but the noisy geese, sacred to Juno, awakened the soldiers. The birds were celebrated for having saved Rome.

a beheaded wolf: Suetonius, in *Tiberius*, XXV, records that Tiberius said that in ruling Rome he was holding a wolf by the ears.

ANGELS GRIEVING OVER THE DEAD CHRIST

The title is from a description of the Thessalonikan epitaphios in *Byzantium*, by Paul Hetherington and Werner Forman (London: Orbis, 1983). Hetherington proposes that the epitaphios, an Orthodox liturgical length of cloth, was worn, perhaps, over the heads of priests as they approached the altar to celebrate the Eucharist. The epitaphios of Thessaloniki was discovered in 1900.

both/God and the worm laughed: I have not been able to locate the source of this legend.

CHRIST DEAD

Mantegna's legendary painting, now in the Brera Gallery in Milan, is variously dated from 1457 to 1500. Although monumental in character and feeling, the painting measures only 68 x 81 cm.

"uncarved block": The source for this image is *The Tao Te Ching* of Lao-Tzu, as translated by Arthur Waley (New York: Grove Press, 1958).

he lay in Sion: Romans 9:33: "I lay in Sion a stumblingstone and rock of offense."

TIBERIUS LEARNS OF THE RESURRECTION

Eusebius records the extraordinary legend, first recounted by Tertullian, that the Emperor Tiberius heard news of the Crucifixion and Resurrection of Jesus in Palestine, that Tiberius was favorably disposed to the story, and that he sought the Senate's approval and confirmation to admit Jesus into the circle of Rome's officially recognized gods. The Senate rejected the Emperor's request.

Dreams his face is carved: According to Tacitus in the *Annals*, IV, xxxvii–xxxviii, Cassius Dio in *Roman History*, LVII, vii–ix, and Suetonius in his *Tiberius*, XXVI, Tiberius famously and repeatedly rejected divine honors for himself; he explicitly forbade that statues and busts of himself be set up without his permission, and when he did permit them, they were to be set up, in the words of Suetonius, "not among the statues of the gods, but as part of the decoration for the temples."

the face of Drusus: In A.D. 33, Tiberius ordered the deaths of Agrippina and her sons Nero and Drusus, all of whom he had earlier banished. The terrors of Drusus' death by starvation are recorded by Tacitus in *Annals*, VI.

Man is a madman clambering: Cassius Dio, in *Roman History*, LVI, xxix: "During a horse-race which took place at the festival of Augustalia, held in honor of Augustus' birthday, a madman seated himself in the chair dedicated to Julius Caesar and, taking his crown, put it on his own head."

These are my temples in your hearts . . . : This is an excerpt from a speech delivered by Tiberius to the Conscript Fathers in A.D. 25, rejecting a request from Farther Spain to erect a shrine to Tiberius and his mother, Livia, as quoted by Tacitus in IV, translated by Naphtali Lewis and Meyer Reinhold in *Roman Civilization, Sourcebook II: The Empire* (New York: Columbia University Press, 1955).

The statue of a god: In *Tiberius*, LXXIV, Suetonius records that Tiberius dreamed of a statue of Apollo on his last birthday.

It is not the Roman custom . . . : Acts of the Apostles 25:16.

Vasari records the story that Piero della Francesca was blind from the age of sixty until his death, according to Vasari, at the age of eighty-six. He also reports that Piero's houses and property were burned and destroyed in the civil strife of 1536, decades after Piero's death.

When you were young, you girded/Yourself...: These are among the last words of the resurrected Jesus in the Gospel of John, 21:18.

THE DREAM OF CONSTANTINE

you saw rivers washing...: Taken from the *Latin Panegyrics*, V, an anonymous fourth-century oration to the Emperor Constantine, translated by Naphtali Lewis and Meyer Reinhold in *Roman Civilization, Sourcebook II: The Empire.*

the nails that fastened His hands: According to the fifth-century Greek historian Socrates Scholasticus in *The Ecclesiastical History*, translated and with notes from Valesius (London: George Bell and Sons, 1874): "Moreover Constantine caused the nails with which Christ's hands were fastened to the Cross (for his mother having found these also in the sepulchre had sent them) to be converted into bridle-bits and a helmet, which he used in his military expeditions."

The secret of the Empire...: Tacitus in *Histories*, I, iv, referring to the death of the Emperor Nero.

a stone that cries out in a wall: Habakkuk 2:11: "For a stone shall cry out from the wall."

We wish this church...: From a summarized text of a letter from the Emperor Constantine to Macarius, Bishop of Jerusalem, about the construction of the Church of the Holy Sepulchre, in the year 326, here translated by Cyril Mango in *Byzantine Architecture* (New York: Rizzoli, 1985), p. 15.

Though your men boil grass: That men out of hunger were driven to boiling straw and drinking the water from it is a legend of the Rabbi Johanan about the siege of Jerusalem, recounted by Chaim Raphael in *The Walls of Jerusalem* (New York: Knopf, 1968), p. 25.

PART THREE/A MONUMENT IN UTOPIA

The epigraph from the Talmud is translated by Olga Marx in Martin Buber, *Tales of the Hasidim: Early Masters* (New York: Schocken Books, 1947). In another translation, in a discussion between Gamaliel and the Sadducees on the resurrection of the dead, Rabbi Johanan is quoted as saying in the name of Rabbi Simeon ben Jehozedek: "When a rule of Law (Halakah) is cited in this world in the name of a dead teacher, his lips move gently in the tomb" (Cant. 7, 10), translated by George Foot Moore, *Judaism in the First Centuries of the Christian*

Era: The Age of the Tannaim, Vol. II (Cambridge: Harvard University Press, 1927), p. 382.

Throughout the poem, references are adapted from phrases and quotations from *Osip Mandelstam: Selected Poems*, translated by Clarence Brown and W. S. Merwin (New York: Atheneum, 1983), especially numbers 235, 267, 272, 306, 307, 329, 341, and 367.

Numerous details and references are adapted from *Hope Against Hope: A Memoir*, by Nadezhda Mandelstam (New York: Atheneum, 1970), including the following: that the first searches of Mandelstam's rooms were carried out by incompetent police interrogators, and that the Mandelstams' papers were stuffed into the most obvious hiding places; that Mandelstam read Alexander Herzen as a schoolboy; that often, even before his final arrest, Mandelstam was not in possession of a proper winter coat; that Mandelstam may have worn a yellow leather coat, which he traded for a half kilo of sugar, in the labor camp; that the word "money," written on a scrap of brown paper in the labor camp in a note asking that warm clothes and money be sent to him, is among the last words Mandelstam wrote; that Mandelstam composed not by writing with a pen or pencil but by whispering the words to himself—moving his lips—and then dictating the poems to Nadezhda Mandelstam.

1

glass panes / Of eternity: See the translation of poem #8 by R. H. Morrison in *Poems from Mandelstam* (Rutherford, N.J.: Fairleigh Dickinson University Press, 1990).

2

the frost's face: See the translation of poem #349 by James Greene in *Osip Mandelstam* (London: Granada Publishing, Paul Elek Ltd., 1980).

3

On the subject of Mandelstam's books and his bookcase, described by Mandelstam in *The Noise of Time*, Nadezhda Mandelstam writes: "In the hope of helping him to survive while his fate was decided, I took a few books from our bookcase and sold them in a secondhand bookstore, and spent the proceeds on the first and only food package I was able to buy for him. It was returned 'because of the death of the addressee'" (*Hope Against Hope*, Chapter 51).

5

childless Petrograd: This is an adaptation of Mandelstam's "childless Byzantium" in his essay *The Nature of the Word*, translated by Jane Gray Harris and Constance Link, in *Mandelstam: The Complete Critical Prose and Letters* (Ann Arbor: Ardis, 1979), p. 120.

Like the Pharaoh's baker: See Genesis 40:16–22.

Who, then, that has lived . . . : This is an ironic paraphrase from Michael Psellus's encomiastic description of the dying days of Emperor Michael IV (1034–41), in Book IV of the *Chronographia,* translated by E.R.A. Sewter (New York: Penguin, 1966).

6

Novgorod is presented, in Mandelstam's poem #235, as an age-old seat of resistance and rebellion against Moscow. In the chapter "A Fur Coat Above One's Station" in *The Noise of Time,* Mandelstam describes the Novgorodians who "used to be depicted as raging on their ikons," translated by Clarence Brown in *The Prose of Osip Mandelstam* (Princeton: Princeton University Press, 1965).

That Stalin was the son of a "devout washerwoman" and a cobbler who "savagely beat" him is from the article on Stalin by Ronald Francis Hingley in the *Encyclopaedia Britannica,* 15th edition.

Doodling wolves in red ink: Reported to be the last observed activity of Stalin, when he was last seen alive by a non-Party member, in James H. Billington, *The Icon and the Axe* (New York: Knopf, 1966), p. 543.

7

They never asked themselves . . . : From somewhere in Edward Gibbon, *The Decline and Fall of the Roman Empire.*

each growing leaf / From the old world: The metaphor of the repression of leaves and the cutting away of branches from the old life is Nadezhda Mandelstam's.

that mound of heads: According to Nadezhda Mandelstam, toward the end of his life Mandelstam was tormented by a recurring fantasy of "hillocks of human heads," as in poem #341. In *Hope Against Hope* Mrs. Mandelstam quotes him as saying, with reference to Stalin: "Whenever I think of him, I see heads, mounds of heads. What is he doing with all those heads?"

Redouté and Josephine: Pierre-Joseph Redouté (1759–1840) was the supreme botanical illustrator of his age, renowned especially for his paintings of roses, many types of which he named as well as painted. The Empress Josephine was one of his many pupils.

INDEX OF TITLES

INDEX OF FIRST LINES